Pumpkins

at

Midnight

A Woman's Guide to Love, Dating,
and Marriage in the Age of Porn

ADAM MOORE, PhD

AND

WENDY MORKEL, MA

SELA BOOKS

Printed by Sela Books, LLC, in the United States of America.

First printing, 2022.

SELA BOOKS
PO BOX 50207
PROVO, UT 84605
WWW.SELABOOKS.COM

ISBN: 978-0-578-37026-2

For the women who've walked this path and wanted more
for their daughters, sisters, and friends.

CONTENTS

INTRODUCTION

The word on the street is that dating is getting painful. Maybe you're anticipating the fourth date with a guy you like, and he ghosts you, never to be heard from again. Or in order to play the game, you have to worry about curating your six social media profiles for maximum appeal, which can make you feel more like a commodity than a human. You have to worry about predators, trolls, and bullies. People don't really get to know each other anymore before making snap decisions about them. Guys are too busy swiping on dating apps to sweep you off your feet.

And then there's pornography.

We live in a porn-saturated world. And some of the guys you date will have experimented with it, while others spend hours a day wasting away in front of it. If you haven't already, you'll likely find that life with a compulsive porn user is anything but a fairy tale. In this book, we'll teach you:

- how porn use can affect a relationship and why you have the right to stand up for your needs
- the panic-free steps to addressing porn use with your partner clearly and compassionately, before hiding or ignoring it becomes a pattern in your relationship
- the tools your partner will need to confront compulsive porn use, and how you can support him
- why it's not your responsibility to fix your partner
- how to make sure you're thriving on your own *and* in your relationship.

Four voices will guide you through this book, each one identified by name:

ADAM

I'm here to help couples who choose to fight a porn habit together by showing you how to sidestep the potholes along the healing path. I have years of experience as a therapist, and I know how to have the tough conversations, deal with painful emotions and experiences, and use the tools that work to kick porn out of your relationship.

WENDY

I let you in on the cutting-edge research about how porn affects people and relationships. You'll also read about my interviews with women who've walked in your shoes—dating or married to a compulsive porn user, wondering if they're making the right choices. You'll also meet men brave enough to share their stories of their own compulsions. You'll follow them all in their search for healthy relationships despite the threat of porn. Their stories will give you the courage to make difficult but rewarding choices, knowing you're not alone.

GENEVIEVE

Genevieve's true story weaves throughout the book and punctuates the principles we teach. Her struggles show how one strong woman can confront pornography as it shows up in her life.

JACOB

You'll also read Jacob's story about his descent into compulsive porn use, which will take you inside the head of a man who longs to change but doesn't know how.

Together, these narrators give you the knowledge and tools to not only navigate one troubling aspect of the dating world today, but also to build a fantastic relationship from the get-go. You'll gain excellent communication skills as well as a transformative under-standing of your own needs. So let's do this.

PART ONE:

THE PRINCESS
AND THE PORN

(defining the problem)

1. THE UNEXPECTED LINK BETWEEN BUTTERFLY WINGS AND PORN

There is no passion to be found in playing small—in settling for a life that is less than the one you are capable of living.
—Nelson Mandela

ADAM

Times have changed. Pornography used to live behind the adults-only curtain in your local video store and in magazines that arrived in the mail, wrapped in opaque plastic. Now any smartphone can be a window into a world of limitless images and videos that offer free and seemingly anonymous sexual stimulation. You can view pornography for hundreds of hours and never come across the same image twice. Not only that, but pornography no longer passively waits to be found. Even if you aren't looking for it, it will be looking for you.[*][1]

---

* In 1998 Dr. Al Cooper described the proliferation of online pornography use as the "Triple-A Engine": standing for "accessibility, affordability, and anonymity." Anyone with home internet access can view pornography privately and for free, which wasn't the case before internet pornography came on the scene.

WENDY

The reality is, the world is saturated in sexual imagery. Most high school students will be exposed to pornography before graduation.[2] By college, more than eight out of ten men and three out of ten women admit to viewing pornography. Two out of ten of those men view it almost every day.[3] Whether we like it or not, porn has infiltrated plenty of people's lives and relationships.

HOW PORN HARMS: SUPERNORMAL STIMULI

To understand how pornography can sabotage a person's natural impulses for love, affection, and sexuality, we need to talk about *supernormal stimuli*. We can thank Nikolaas Tinbergen for discovering supernormal stimuli. Tinbergen was an interesting guy: a Dutch boy at the turn of the twentieth century who'd rather daydream and roam the countryside than focus on his studies. So of course he shocked everyone when he survived life as a World War II POW and grew up to be a Nobel-prize-winning physiologist and biologist, a pioneer in fields ranging from autism to instinct to natural and abnormal development. Niko Tinbergen got stuff done.

What I'm getting at comes from Tinbergen's research on instinct in the 1950s. Tinbergen had a gift for creative experimentation. Curious about how physical appearance affects animals' response to fellow members of their species, he made larger-than-life bird eggs out of plaster and amplified their markings. He put the giant polka-dot eggs in the nest next to the normal eggs, and surprise— the mama birds chose to sit on the fakes and neglect their real babies.

Any good scientist knows he needs to replicate his study in order to verify the results, so Tinbergen performed a similar experiment with butterfly mating. He made cardboard female butterflies with ornate wing markings and set them among a butterfly colony. Guess what happened? Yep, the male butterflies attempted to mate with the lifeless cut-outs and rejected the flesh-and-blood (or rather, membrane-and-hemolymph) females.

In a nutshell, that's a supernormal stimulus: a physical feature that's exaggerated beyond the natural world and hijacks our biological response. Male butterflies are attracted to females by the markings on their wings, but when the markings are unnatural and over the top, the males prefer the fakes, even though they have neither mating nor companionship to offer.

Pornography is a supernormal stimulus for humankind. When you watch pornography, you see some pretty extreme bodies and behaviors, just like those bling-winged cardboard butterflies. On a purely instinctive level, it might look appealing, but it's a hollow charade—a tripped-out, smoke-and-mirrors mirage. It lacks the vulnerable, affectionate, human element that can make sex wonderful. And sadly, people who regularly watch pornography begin to substitute that oversize illusion for real intimacy.[4]

And porn really can be a drug. In recent neuroimaging studies, neurologists have found that the brains of people who identify as compulsive users respond to pornography in the same ways smokers' and heroin users' brains respond to their drug of choice, which we'll discuss further in Chapter Three. However, it isn't porn use alone that is likely to create this rewiring of the brain.[*][5]

PORN USE AND MASTURBATION

Pornography use typically isn't casual or passive. Most compulsive users aren't getting together with their buddies to watch some porn. They're watching alone and in secret while masturbating. And whether or not they want to, over time this combination of behaviors can train a brain to be aroused by sex on a screen, sometimes at the expense of sex with a real person.

Masturbation itself hasn't been proven to be psychologically harmful.[6] But when you combine porn use with the powerful feelings masturbation elicits, there's evidence that this combination can rewire a brain's sexual response, at least temporarily. Thousands of men claim it's happened to them.[7]

The late neurologist Gary Wilson's website yourbrainonporn. com is dedicated to helping people—mostly young men—give up

---

* Compared to non-addicts, frequent porn users have a quicker and more heightened response when they see a pornographic image, they are more likely to seek novel images than non-addicts, and they experience more cravings but less enjoyment than infrequent users when shown a pornographic image.

masturbating to pornography so that they can have an active sex life with a real person, because they aren't able to do both. On Wilson's site, over 4500 people report persistent sexual problems when trying to be intimate with someone—problems that don't exist when watching porn—such as erectile dysfunction, low libido, and inability to maintain arousal. Remember, these aren't geriatric men. They're typically in their teens, twenties, and thirties. If that isn't enough on its own, many also complain of social and emotional problems that have arisen since watching porn, such as anxiety, depression, low self-confidence, inability to focus, and other mental health issues. The supernormal stimulus of porn coupled with the power of orgasm packs a potent punch that can knock a person out. And when an individual is suffering, their relationships suffer too.

YOUR NEEDS MATTER

ADAM

Pornography exposure doesn't always devolve into compulsive use. But when it does, porn users often minimize the seriousness of the problem. Too often, couples avoid discussing pornography use, hoping in vain that it's a non-issue, so they don't recognize how it's affecting their relationship until years later, when their marriage is strained to its breaking point.

You've probably heard Benjamin Franklin's famous wisdom: "Keep your eyes wide open before marriage, half shut afterwards." Learning to keep your eyes half shut will be a great tool to help both of you become more open-minded and love each other, flaws and all. After you're married, choose your battles wisely. Part of marriage is learning to chill out and let go of some of your hangups. Maybe he'll leave the toilet seat up or snore like a grizzly bear.

You might get used to his other habits, but problematic pornography use often creates too much pain to ignore. Confronting porn will mean more to your life together than which way you load the toilet paper onto the holder or whether you'll let your kids dye their hair weird colors.

As a therapist, I see people in incredible pain. They've tried everything to stop the cycle of pornography use and deceit. I often meet couples when the wife can't take it anymore. She tells her husband that she's tried to support him for years, hoping he'll overcome the porn use. She's believed in him. She's hoped that someday this problem would vanish and they could be happy.

Then one day, she realizes nothing has changed. He needs help. They need help. But he's been using porn compulsively for so long that he can't understand why she's upset. Often he even blames her for their problems. When they first come into my office, I can see in their faces years of trauma, sadness, and loss.

I know that we can't prevent all pain. Life is hard. That said, your marriage is worth protecting. You have a right to ask your future husband important questions, expect him to be honest, and master the tools to help you defend your relationship from the effects of pornography. In the following chapters, Wendy and I will give you the tools to stand up for your needs, talk openly and honestly about pornography, and work as a team to develop a close, connected relationship unshackled from pornography.

JACOB   APRIL 1997

Minutes tick by like hours in the silent house as Jacob's throat burns while he lies in bed, not sick enough to drift off into delirium. "Just stay home—better safe than sorry," his mom decided before leaving for work, promising to take him to the walk-in clinic that evening. It's fine with Jacob. With a 4.0 GPA and a mint-condition 1390 on his pre-SAT, Jacob can afford to miss a day or two of school. He wasn't really looking forward to another endless day feeling invisible among his peers anyway. Maybe he's less lonely when he's alone.

When he's sure sleep won't come, Jacob kicks his gangly legs out of bed. He feels a tug down the dark hall toward his parents' room but wills himself to turn right and head toward the family room in the open end of the house. He flips on the Nintendo 64 and grabs his controller. He's already beaten each of the five games he owns, but maybe he can try to win *Super Mario 64* without dying. Twenty minutes in, he's devoured by a piranha plant in a part that should've been easy.

Jacob shrugs and switches off the console then starts flipping through the channels on TV, settling on an episode of *Judge Judy*. A lady stands behind a podium and howls, mascara running down her face, while a man towers behind another podium, rolling his eyes now and then. Something about a broken lease and a towed car. Jacob shuts off the TV. He looks in the cabinet next to the TV for a movie to watch. Just a bunch of *Moonlighting* episodes his mom recorded. And *ET*, which he can recite by memory.

Where's that box of black-and-white movies? With Cary Grant, Humphrey Bogart, all the great ones? Jacob used to fall asleep watching them with his dad. They were in this cabinet for years. He digs through the old newspapers and coffee-table books in the cabinet, but the box isn't there. Maybe they're in his dad's closet?

He heads back down the hall and into his parents' room. No box of films in the closet. Folded sweaters, a tub full of earrings, stacks of his dad's *Road and Track* magazines. He puts it all back and shuts the door.

As he passes his mom's nightstand, he pauses, feeling her Sears Christmas catalog tug at him from inside the drawer. The hours he poured over those images of women standing in beige underwear come flooding back.

No. Not anymore. That was the old Jacob. It's been, what, maybe two weeks since he decided he was done with that? If his mom and dad knew... He bites his lower lip and shoves his hands in his pockets, rushing past the nightstand.

What about the kitchen? He gives the pantry a quick once-over. No luck. He checks the cupboards above the kitchen desk, the shelves too close together to house a box of videos. But he unpacks them anyway. In one stack of papers and bills is an issue of *Vogue*. He's looked through it before. He opens the magazine and scans the women on each page.

It's not like he's doing anything wrong. They're wearing clothing. Well, some aren't wearing a lot of it.

Jacob feels a little sick and alive all at once. When he's seen every photo twice, he places everything back where it was, both the organized and the disheveled, even laying an errant hair back on top of the stack that holds the magazine.

As he climbs off the desk chair, a white envelope on the island catches his eye. Internal Revenue Service. Jacob snaps back to reality. Didn't Mom ask Matt to put it in the mail on his way out to his girlfriend's house last night? Guess he forgot. If he's not mistaken about what Mr. Myers said in Civics, April 15th is always tax day. Which is today.

Jacob opens the front door and sees the mail truck at the mailbox. In the same moment he glimpses his disheveled hair in the mirror to the left at the entryway. He looks down at his bare feet and too-short pajama pants. He closes his eyes and takes a deep breath. If anyone sees him like this... But he runs out the front door anyway.

The mail truck pulls away. Oh, sheesh.

Jacob runs out into the road. When the mail truck pulls up at the house next door, Jacob comes to an immediate stop between the driver's side of the truck and the Murphys' mailbox, waving the letter in the air for the postal worker to see. She sees him and flinches. Jacob grimaces. Suddenly he wants nothing more than to sink into the asphalt.

"Sorry. I was hoping you could take this," he mutters.

The mail lady looks at the envelope, then back up at Jacob. She smiles at him. "Oh, yeah! Your parents will be glad you caught me."

"Thanks." Jacob hangs his head and turns back toward home. His temples pound.

He makes his way through the front door. What now? Images from that stupid catalog in the nightstand stream through his mind as this interminable day stretches out before him. He clenches his jaw.

Right. The classic films. He could search the garage. He heads out to the garage, his throat still burning from his neighborhood jaunt. He digs through tarps and tents, hammers and hacksaws. No dice. Cardboard boxes sit on shelves on the far wall of the garage. Jacob's never seen inside of any of them. One box has a bunch of paperwork. The next one holds books.

In an unlabeled box on the highest shelf on the far wall of the garage, Jacob strikes forbidden gold. Not the old movies. Something else. His chest tingles, spreading to his face and fingers. About a dozen *Playboy* magazines are neatly stacked inside the box. The only time he's stumbled on anything close was the images that popped up on Uncle Greg's computer when he was playing an online game at his house. Jacob's heart pounds, hardly believing that this unholy grail was right out here in the garage.

And then, out of nowhere Jacob almost starts to wonder how the contraband came into his home. A flash of worry for a fraction of a second. About his dad, or maybe Matt, about what secrets of their own one of them might be hiding. But then the feeling vanishes. And then another flash—a fleeting sense that something is terribly wrong with him. But then that half-feeling again disappears before it even registers.

Right there, perched on the wobbly stepladder under the light of a single exposed bulb, Jacob disappears into another world. Exhilaration drowns out everything else. The sore throat. The kids who ignore him. His paralysis every time he longs to belong, to talk to people, worried he'll say something dumb. The way he feels every single thing *too much*. For a few minutes, Jacob escapes into an illusion where he has attention, admiration, relevance. Something that he might mistake for happiness, if he thought about it. Or maybe love.

But then that electricity dissolves like cotton candy wisps, and he's suddenly numb. On autopilot. Turning page after page like a zombie.

The first ring of the phone in the kitchen doesn't register. By the second ring, he jolts back to earth, his pulse racing. He looks around the garage. Is someone watching him? Should he answer the phone? It might be Mom. She'll wonder what's wrong if he doesn't pick up.

He jumps off the stepladder, races to the door, and grabs the phone from its cradle by the fourth ring.

"Hello?" he pants, then holds his breath, hoping the caller

doesn't sense anything amiss.

"Jacob. Sweetie. Are you all right?" Sure enough.

"Oh. Hi, Mom." Jacob's face feels hot. "Yeah. I'm good."

"Honey, I just remembered—I don't think Matt put our tax returns in the mailbox. The mail lady usually comes at 12:30, so—"

"The mail lady came already. I gave her the envelope."

"We need to get it postmarked today. It's a white envelope on the kitchen—"

"Mom. I said I gave it to the mail lady."

"You did?"

"I saw it on the island. I saw it like an hour ago. I ran after the mail truck to chase her down."

"Oh, sweetie. Really?"

"I did."

"Oh! Thank you! I'd have to come home and take it to the post office, and I can't take any more time off work."

"No problem."

"You don't sound great."

"Mom. I'm fine. It's just a sore throat."

"You sound out of breath. Like you were running around."

Jacob's palms sweat, and his ears start ringing. He rubs his forehead with his free hand. "I was playing Nintendo. I had to pause the game and run to get the phone."

"Oh, honey, don't play too many games. It's not good for you. Why don't you get some homework done?"

"My head's all foggy. I can't do homework right now."

"Oh, that's not good. Maybe I should ask Dad if he can come home and take you to the clinic."

"No, I'm okay. I'm fine. My homework is caught up anyway."

"Okay... Well, can I run and pick you up some cough syrup after work?"

"Mom! Stop worrying! I can take care of myself."

The line is silent.

Jacob winces.

"Okay. I'm sorry, sweetie."

More silence.

"Well, just try to get some rest," she timidly adds.

"It's okay, Mom. Just... Please don't worry about me. I'm fine. I'll go lie down."

"Okay, bye, sweetie."

Jacob lays the phone in its cradle, exhaling. Why does he always hurt her feelings? She wouldn't understand, even if he told her about his searches, about the magazines. Nobody would. Anyway, he might die if she knew.

He looks around the room, feeling weird in his own skin. Okay. He can fix this. Maybe... Maybe he just needs to eat. He grabs a jar of peanut butter and a loaf of bread from the pantry and makes a sandwich. He takes a bite, swallowing as it sears his sore throat. He needed to eat. That's all.

In the middle of his fifth bite, a chill passes down his spine. He remembers the magazine lying open on the stepladder, thinks of his mom's Volvo pulling into the garage at 5:00 sharp. Or earlier, if she changes her mind about coming to check on him. He drops the sandwich on the counter and races back out to the garage. He closes the magazine, averting his eyes toward the wall, and lays it in the box. Then he puts both hands inside the box on either side of the magazines to adjust the stack, aligns all the edges, and examines his work to see if he's left any evidence. As he starts to replace the lid, he feels another tug. Maybe just one more quick look.

He opens the magazine at the top of the stack and disappears again, defeated and numb. The electricity has gone out of him, and now there's nothing at all. Not the pain of hurting Mom if she knew. No more hopelessness. No more worry that he's bad, or broken somehow. He turns page after page, a shell of Jacob. No longer the achiever, the big dreamer, not the one who longs to be accepted. He's only here, in this moment. And yet he's not even here. He's not anywhere.

1 Cooper, Al. "Sexuality and the Internet: Surfing into the new millennium." *CyberPsychology & Behavior* 1, no. 2 (1998): 187-193.

2 Chiara Sabina, Janis Wolak, and David Finkelhor, "The nature and dynamics of internet pornography exposure for youth," *CyberPsychology and Behavior* 11 (2008): 691-693.

3 Jason S. Carroll, Laura M. Padilla-Walker, Larry J. Nelson, Chad D. Olson, Carolyn McNamara Barry, and Stephanie D. Madsen, "Generation XXX: Pornography acceptance and use among emerging adults." *Journal of Adolescent Research* 23 (2008): 6-30.

4 Love, Todd, Christian Laier, Matthias Brand, Linda Hatch, and Raju Hajela. "Neuroscience of Internet pornography addiction: A review and update." *Behavioral Sciences* 5, no. 3 (2015): 388-433.

5 Love, Todd, Christian Laier, Matthias Brand, Linda Hatch, and Raju Hajela. "Neuroscience of Internet Pornography Addiction: A Review and Update." *Behavioral Sciences* 5, no. 3 (2015): 388-433.

Voon, Valerie, Thomas B. Mole, Paula Banca, Laura Porter, Laurel Morris, Simon Mitchell, Tatyana R. Lapa et al. "Neural correlates of sexual cue reactivity in individuals with and without compulsive sexual behaviours." *PloS one* 9, no. 7 (2014): e102419.

Brand, Matthias, Jan Snagowski, Christian Laier, and Stefan Maderwald. "Ventral striatum activity when watching preferred pornographic pictures is correlated with symptoms of Internet pornography addiction."

NeuroImage 129 (2016): 224-232.

Banca, Paula, Laurel S. Morris, Simon Mitchell, Neil A. Harrison, Marc N. Potenza, and Valerie Voon. "Novelty, conditioning and attentional bias to sexual rewards." *Journal of Psychiatric Research* 72 (2016): 91-101.

6   Coleman, Eli. "Masturbation as a means of achieving sexual health." *Journal of Psychology & Human Sexuality* 14, no. 2-3 (2003): 5-16.

7   Wilson, Gary. *Your Brain on Porn: Internet Pornography and the Emerging Science of Addiction.* Margate, Kent, United Kingdom: Commonwealth Publishing, 2017.

2. YOU DESERVE GOOD THINGS

Pay attention to the wound. That's where the light gets in.
    —the Buddha

WENDY

Some of the most powerful and compassionate people in history have a story born in struggle: Helen Keller, Joan of Arc, Maya Angelou, Oprah Winfrey. Ugliness that gives birth to beauty is a tale that spans the globe.

Musicians compose dark, dissonant chords that transform into bright harmonies in the next beat. That change feels satisfying, almost transcendent. Cultures around the world tell of a sacred bird, the phoenix, reborn from its own ashes. And then there's the hero's journey, found in stories from ancient myths to modern novels, where an ordinary person must leave their small life and face obstacle after unbearable obstacle until they learn what they must to become the hero they were meant to be.

Even fairy tales, often dismissed for being too cheesy and saccharine, have struggle woven into their fabric. Sure, I've never had a fairy godmother give me an exquisite gown and a regal coach to whisk me away to a night of luxury and romance. But remember, that's not the whole story. When the clock strikes twelve, Cinderella's coach morphs into pumpkins, her dress to rags, and she has to face a dreary life with an abusive stepfamily in order to fight for true love.

The musician, the phoenix, and the heroine all play an active role in overcoming pain. They *use* suffering and strife to build or become something changed and beautiful. And now or later, this will be your story too.

YOU HAVE MORE POWER THAN YOU KNOW

ADAM

Wendy and I are going to ask you to do some hard things. And that might sound scary. I've heard some of my clients say: "What if I stand up for myself, and then nobody likes me, and I die alone?" I'm paraphrasing here, but maybe you're afraid that if you push too hard for your own needs, you'll drive the people you love away. The bad news: that's a risk. But the good news is that it's a risk worth taking. Yes, the users and abusers may disappear, but the people who really matter will stick around.

So I'm asking you to trust me. If you don't know it yet, at least trust that you're worth sacrificing for. Trust that your challenges don't mean there's something wrong with you. They just mean that life is hard.

As a therapist, I meet brave and resilient women every day, women who annihilate obstacles to create the lives they want— obstacles like the grief, uncertainty, and isolation that often come with a partner's pornography use. I've worked with enough of these fighters to know that you too are capable of that superhuman inner strength and compassion, whether you realize it or not.

I've also noticed that women seem driven, whether by biology or culture, to be very hard on themselves in an effort to become the best version of themselves they can be. And there's a growing field of evidence backing up this notion.

WENDY

Maybe you've heard that girls outperform boys in school. You can argue that our schools don't cater to the ways boys learn— they'd rather run around outside than sit still at a desk. But there's more to it than that. In developed nations, girls spend an average of 5.5 hours per week on homework, while boys spend just 4.2.[1] And when authors Katty Kay and Claire Shipman interviewed powerful women in high corporate positions,[2] they were surprised to find that these movers and shakers were plagued by self-doubt.

Then there's Hewlett Packard's accidental insight into the pressure women place on themselves: When HP reviewed personnel records to investigate why the megacorporation didn't employ more women in top management positions, they found that women only applied for a promotion if they met 100% of the criteria for the job. Men applied if they met just sixty percent of the same criteria.[3] Today's women strive for excellence, while at the same time they're plagued by overwhelming insecurities.

What's more, our culture has been telling you the weirdest lies about yourself, probably for most of your life. Likely from your earliest years, you've been bombarded with images of women with "perfect" (translation: heavily airbrushed and surgically altered) bodies, exuding sexuality, sending the misguided memo that

1. As a woman, physical beauty is the primary indicator of your worth.
2. Being different from these images makes you substandard.
3. You are a sexual object.

So as women, we have to fight just to like ourselves for the smart, capable, gloriously imperfect people we are. In order to overcome the hurdles we address in this book, you'll have to ignore the naysayers and the voice inside your head that tells you you're not good enough.

TRUE LOVE'S KISS WON'T FIX HIM

ADAM

In addition to standing up for your needs like a boss, you'll have to contend with infatuation while you're making decisions about marriage. When you fall in love, you'll probably have two simultaneous experiences: At times you'll worry about the future. You might wonder, "Will I be a good wife?" "Will my husband be a good man?" "Am I making the right decisions?"

But at other times, you'll also suffer from infatuation. This means that your rational brain will all but shut down. Your fears might just disappear into the ether, and you'll feel like love will conquer all, as if the world is bursting with sunshine and puppies and rainbows. That's what infatuation does.

Giving up the "I can do what I want, when I want" single life in order to permanently tether ourselves to another human being sounds pretty illogical if you think about it, so it's almost a miracle that infatuation gives us a swift kick in the pants to carry on the species. But infatuation can also be a deceptive little monster. It keeps us from making the self-preserving decisions we'd make if our brains weren't orbiting Jupiter.

On top of the infatuation issue, many women have strong caretaking instincts, which can cross over into their relationships and marriages. Some women see would-be red flags in a man and think, "He just needs all my love, and he will change." You might believe that your love alone can cure your future husband of any faults that he may have.

Don't make that mistake when it comes to his pornography use. You can't cure compulsive pornography use with only kindness and enduring love. In order to break a pornography habit, you first have to talk about it. If porn becomes an issue in your marriage (which happens far too often), avoiding the topic won't make it go away.

VERBALIZE YOUR NEEDS

I want to help you become fearless about discussing pornography.

Some problems matter more than others. Pornography matters. I've seen it ruin too many marriages to deny that. And this skill will help you stand up for your needs in many ways in your marriage.

When my wife and I were engaged, we started to merge our money. We stopped making individual financial decisions and started asking each other about whether we should buy this or that. This might not be a good idea for everyone, but we felt confident that this relationship was "the one."

So one evening, she and I were eating dinner at a cafe. We had invited my parents to join us for the evening—maybe to get some wisdom about marriage. The conversation turned to a surround sound audio system I wanted to buy as my last significant purchase before marriage. It was expensive. I was talking it up and watching the expression on my fiancée's face.

Suddenly, right in the middle of talking about decibels and wattage, I realized something. To my great horror, I understood: *She is not going to let me buy this system. She thinks it's a waste of money. She has no intention of owning this monstrosity.*

At this point I threw what I can only describe as an adult tantrum. I was whining, begging, moaning that she was being unfair. I know for sure that I wasn't attractive to my future wife at that moment. I turned to my parents, hoping for some kind of rescue. They looked at me as if to say, "Sorry, man. Welcome to married life."

I finally calmed down and learned something important: things were going to change forever. I was marrying a woman who wouldn't just let me do whatever I wanted. I'm grateful now—very grateful. At the time, I probably wasn't all that grateful.

It may seem insignificant, but my wife had the courage to stand up for what mattered to her, such as making wise choices as a couple about the little money we had. She was smart enough to know that ignoring serious issues like finances wouldn't make them go away.

Right now, talking about pornography with a guy you're dating may sound awkward or even a little ridiculous. And maybe it's not time to bring it up yet. We'll talk about when it's the right time in Chapter Four. And we'll show you how to have that conversation in Chapters Five through Eight. But when the time comes, having honest conversations about pornography can change the trajectory of your relationship.

BECOMING AWARE OF YOUR NEEDS

You may also find throughout this process that at times your emotions regarding pornography use are more powerful than you expected--as if there's more going on underneath the surface. This may be exactly what's happening. Your current distress could be exacerbated by factors beyond your relationship. Years before you met your partner, it's possible that experience taught you the world couldn't be trusted. And now, finding out that the person you're supposed to be closest to and feel safe with secretly uses pornography? You suddenly find yourself engulfed in those old, buried emotions as if you're feeling them for the first time.

As children, we were vulnerable and relatively powerless. Life happened to us--and sometimes what happened could be quite distressing. Experiences ranging from a parent's job loss, Mom and Dad's marital conflict, having to trust imperfect and unpredictable adults for our well-being, moving or changing schools multiple times, the cruelty of siblings or other children (and even adults), or just struggling to make friends can have longer-lasting effects than we sometimes realize.

These experiences can leave us feeling perpetually defective, unsafe, powerless, or that we're responsible for other people's actions, thoughts, or emotions.[*][4] We'll discuss how each of these wounds develop and what to do about them in Chapter Fourteen. But for now, keep in mind that very strong reactions to a porn problem may signify a pattern of unmet needs that extends way back to your childhood or adolescence.

In many cases, the more powerful the emotional response to pornography, the more powerful the unmet need is in your life. As a child, you may not have known how to stand up for yourself. Or maybe no one listened when you did. It can be empowering to find that voice as an adult. And understanding and voicing your unmet

---

* Francine Shapiro, the creator of EMDR therapy, has proposed that all of our issues boil down to four underlying wounds that originate in childhood and persist into adulthood.

needs will become a crucial predictor of how well the two of you discuss and confront pornography as a team.

So get comfortable with the idea of talking about your needs regarding pornography. Once you're comfortable, I'll help you become fearless. A fearless woman is a force to be reckoned with.

I believe in extraordinary marriages. I'm not interested in facilitating mediocre ones. And no one is going to make an extraordinary marriage for you. You get to do that for yourself. One way you'll do that is by standing up for what really matters to you.

I want future generations of women to be empowered with the knowledge, tools, and self-respect to expect that the men they marry will take the threat of pornography seriously. I want them to have open conversations about porn before marriage and expect to challenge this threat head-on as a team.

I hope you gain the courage to do just that. Stand up for what matters to you. Make conversations about pornography and your future marriage a priority. Don't settle for less than that. Remember, you're worth it.

GENEVIEVE   JULY 2002

Genevieve has a plan.

The old hardwood floor chills her knees, even in the balmy heat of her unair-conditioned bedroom. Three piles of clothes sit before her: to sort, to keep, and to sell or donate. Each time she picks up a blouse, a well-loved pair of jeans, her faded *J'adore Paris* t-shirt from junior high, she squeezes her eyes shut, bracing herself for the choice she *must* make.

In a family where abundance and scarcity alternate like the weather, with a lot more rain than shine, Genevieve clings to anything that is hers. Trinkets. Birthday cards. Hand-me-downs from her older brothers that aren't her style and don't fit anyway. And now she has to let them go. In less than two months, life begins. She'll be catching a ride with a friend of a friend to the

University of Oklahoma, and there won't be space in the Jeep for more than the bare necessities.

While her other school friends brag about their acceptance letters to prestigious universities in picturesque locales, Genevieve's choice suits her just fine. It meets her two criteria: She can afford it with the money she's saved working as a grocery cashier over the past three years—full-time, even during the school year. And it's nearly a thousand miles from home.

As she sorts, the familiar rhythm of her parents' bickering rises from downstairs: her mom's shrieks and her dad's excuses, punctuated by the slam of a drawer. Her mom must be feeling better today. Well, up to a fight, at least.

Genevieve hears her name among the muffled shouts. She balls up the "to keep" pile in her arms and hurls it across the room to calm the lion inside of her, awake at the sound of her own name.

More than once Genevieve has stayed up at the kitchen table late into the night after work, enduring her own screaming match with her parents about leaving. *We are a family! What about us? Don't you love your mother?* Though it changes neither of her parents' minds to retort that normal kids in normal families go away to college, thank you very much, Genevieve always stands her ground. She's eighteen now, a free agent, even if not by her mom and dad's smothering standards.

She's saved up a year's tuition, and she'll earn everything else she needs while she's working at school. She's paid her dues, contributing to her mother's medical bills that can't be covered on her dad's school teacher salary: the doctors' visits, the labs, the hospital stays that only provide more questions about her mom's whole-body pain, her weakness, her debilitating exhaustion. And she's always looked out for Mara, who's only fourteen and can't anticipate Mom's outbursts. Genevieve even helped with payments on the Lexus, the sole family car that her dad should have known they couldn't afford. And little help that was. The beautiful car was repossessed two weeks ago.

Another slam of a door, and then silence. Maybe the trouble has passed. Genevieve needs to leave for work now if she wants to catch the bus on time. She ditches the half-sorted piles and races downstairs to an empty kitchen. She steps out the front door, turns down the cracked path, and almost collides with a shiny blue Ford Explorer on the driveway.

It could be anyone's. Maybe one of her brothers' friends came to visit? But Dad is walking around the side, examining it.

"Whose car is that, Dad?" Genevieve asks, her breath thin.

He stops walking and inhales, his chest growing full, looking Genevieve in the eye. "Genevieve, I know you've saved up all this money to leave us and go off to college, but I looked it up. Tuition isn't due until October eighth. That's almost three months away."

"What— What does college have to do with this car?"

"Listen, Jenny—John Cooper is going to pay me for all the roofing I did for him last summer. He just needs a few more homes to sell before he's in the black. He'll for sure have the money to me by October. And we need a car now. We can't get a loan. Not after the repo. We'd have to come up with the entire $29,000 to get the Lexus back. But there was $10,000 in your account."

The yard starts to spin. All of her money was in that savings account. She blinks once. Her eyes sting. *Of course he took it.*

"Jenny, the car was only nine grand. It was a good deal. There's still a few hundred left in your account. I promise I'll pay it all back as soon as money comes in. Real soon."

She clenches her teeth. "It's Genevieve, Dad."

Genevieve tries to shake off the lion growing inside. John has owed her dad thousands of dollars for over a year now. But this has happened before in other ways. That windfall is always on its way, just around the corner. Maybe if Genevieve rushes to the bank, she can reverse the charges. She can fix his mistake.

No. It was a shared account. The bank won't count it as fraud. The lion rises inside her again. Her ears flush red, her head pulsates. Heat wells inside her.

Her future where everyone's life doesn't bleed into everyone else's, where Genevieve imagined she might live a steady existence on her own terms, has just crumbled into nothing more than a pretty dream. Her head feels like it's going to pound out of her wet, wild eyeballs. True to her upbringing, Genevieve unleashes the roaring lion and lets the screams fly.

1   OECD (2015), *The ABC of Gender Equality in Education: Aptitude, Behaviour, Confidence,* PISA, OECD Publishing. http://dx.doi.org/10.1787/9789264229945-en

2   Shipman, Claire, and Katty Kay. *Womenomics: Write Your Own Rules for Success: How to Stop Juggling and Struggling and Finally Start Living and Working the Way You Really Want.* New York: Harper Business, 2009.

3   Kay, Katty and Claire Shipman. "The Confidence Gap," *The Atlantic, May* 2014. Accessed October 12, 2016. http://www.theatlantic.com/magazine/archive/2014/05/the-confidence-gap/359815/.

4   Shapiro, Francine. *Eye Movement Desensitization and Reprocessing: Basic Principles, Protocols, and Procedures. 2nd edition.* New York: Guilford Press, 2001.

3. THE GHOST OF PORNOGRAPHY FUTURE: YOUR RELATIONSHIP ON PORN

"Bah," said Scrooge. "Humbug."
 —Charles Dickens, *A Christmas Carol*

WENDY

Okay, we're putting on *A Christmas Carol: Marriage Edition*.

You know the drill: Ebenezer Scrooge is a crotchety old miser who doesn't know how lost and lonely he is. Three ghosts visit him on Christmas Eve: the Ghosts of Christmas Past, Present, and Future. They each show him a portion of his life and what it means about his choices. The first two ghosts are friendly enough, even though they don't pull any punches showing Scrooge the relationships he's missed out on. But the third ghost is eerie. Faceless and mute, the ominous Ghost of Christmas Future points his skeletal hand at the horrors yet to come in Scrooge's life.

You can think of me as that spooky creature right now. I'll show you what your *other* future may look like—the one where you don't address porn with your future husband. I'll draw on research about the ways porn affects brains and relationships, as well as interviews with people who've been down this path. And remember, in the end Scrooge takes the ghosts' messages to heart before time runs out. You can too.

Please keep in mind, empirical research doesn't sentence you to a certain outcome. We're more than numbers on a page. Twentieth-century film star George Burns smoked cigars like a chimney and never quit. He lived to be a hundred. But I doubt any doctor would recommend that you take up smoking for your health and longevity. You're often better off safe than sorry when facing the unknown. So let's look at the future that may await if you put your head in the sand regarding porn.

YOUR SEX LIFE

When you're on the verge of marriage, you're in love. You're twitterpated. Maybe you can't bear to be more than a foot away from each other. You won't be unusual if your sex life is what you two are looking forward to most. Even if sex isn't top priority to you, healthy sex has been found to create strong bonds in a relationship, cementing your connection and closeness.

And how might porn hijack your sex life? First of all, you run the risk of rarely having sex if the porn persists. This is all over the research about how porn use affects couples. When one member of a couple uses porn, both sex itself and even the desire for sex with one another *decreases*.[1] One study found that in almost seventy percent of unions where one partner uses porn, one or both partners had lost interest in sex with each other.[2] Seventy percent.

Take the real-world example of Maggie, a woman I interviewed. Maggie was married at thirty. Done with school, employed, and ready to start a family, Maggie didn't worry much about the fact that she and her husband had only dated for four months before the wedding. "I would have seen the behavior if we had dated for longer," she reassures herself as we talk in her midwifery office.

I'm admiring her pink mohawk, a punk-rock emblem she dons as a breast cancer survivor, and her vibrant. empowering attitude toward life. But the events she's describing took place before all of that, when her hair was curly and black and she knew less of life's troubles.

Maggie knew Brad years before they dated. Once they decided to take the plunge, things moved quickly. They seemed happy. They were certainly attracted to each other, at least. They chose to wait until marriage to have sex, but they had a hard time keeping their hands off each other.

But everything changed when they got married. Brad stopped initiating sex after their wedding night. Maggie, never a wallflower, would push Brad for intimacy and be turned down. Maggie was hurt. She'd always heard that men were insatiable sex maniacs. Was Brad just shy?

A few months later, Maggie picked up the mail with the key that Brad usually controlled like a prison warden. As she opened the credit card bill at their kitchen table, she found that Brad had run up over $800 in charges for online pornography. In a single month.

Maggie felt cheated on. She didn't want to share her husband with porn. She tried all of the typical solutions (counseling with church clergy, couples therapy), but in the end Brad was too deep in his porn habit, too unwilling to address his problems. After Brad was fired from his job for watching hours of porn at work each day, and as Brad continued to numb out with porn even as their baby daughter lay in the hospital from a life-threatening emergency, Maggie knew she was done with the marriage. In the end, after ten years of marriage, Maggie and Brad had had sex a total of *six times*. That's a lonely marriage to endure.

Not all stories are a sex vacuum like Maggie's. Some women have a robust sex life with a porn user in terms of sheer quantity, but it isn't the romantic intimacy they dreamed of. Porn, even mainstream porn, isn't simply a natural display of sex and love, a healthy outlet for the sexually enlightened. Pornography these days is cruel and violent. It's a terrible sex educator.

Nearly ninety percent of scenes in pornographic videos portray physical aggression of some sort, ninety-five percent of those violent acts are perpetrated against women, and maybe most sadly, a paltry ten percent of scenes depict any loving or affectionate behavior. [3] Today's porn is cold, violent, misogynistic, and just plain ugly.

When that type of porn enters your bedroom, it can deplete real connection. One study of young male porn users (eighteen to twenty-nine years old) revealed that the more porn a man watched, the more likely he was to try to re-create the unaffectionate, male-centric sex he'd seen in pornography.[4] The frequent porn users also needed to think about the porn instead of focusing on their partner to stay aroused. And the kicker: the more porn men viewed, the less they enjoyed real sex.

What's more, if your partner continues to watch pornography, his porn use might escalate to acting out in the real world. One study found that pornography users, even when both partners voluntarily watched porn together, were twice as likely to cheat on their partners than people who didn't view porn.[5] Other studies have found that porn users are more likely than those who abstain to be unfaithful to their partners in a variety of ways, from flirting to full-blown adultery.[6] Unbridled porn use may be a catalyst for infidelity.

YOUR PERSONAL WELL-BEING

It doesn't sound fair, but *his* pornography use could affect your well-being.

Discovering someday that your husband has secretly been using porn can traumatize you. You might end up with PTSD.[7] Yep, post-traumatic stress disorder, the same condition that shell-shocked war veterans and survivors of violent events develop. PTSD can make you skittish, on edge, hypervigilant, anxious, depressed. It can make you question your reality. It can torpedo your self-esteem.

Maybe it sounds extreme to lump together women who have discovered their husbands' pornography use and those who've survived military combat. But it turns out that PTSD doesn't have to be caused by a physical event like a car accident or an explosion. Trauma is caused by any disturbing experience that is beyond your capacity to cope with. Trauma is contextual and deeply personal. *Emotional* trauma is just as real as physical trauma.

ADAM

Here's what I've learned about trauma from treating women who've experienced it: the pornography use is problematic, but it's the accompanying deceit that most often traumatizes women.

A lot of married guys who are into porn don't want to get caught. So they lie and tell their wives that they're porn-free. When wives start to suspect something is wrong (because women tend to have keen intuition about these things), porn users try to shift the blame back to their wives. "You must be crazy," they say. "Nothing is wrong. Your mind is playing tricks on you." Pretty soon, these women—who want to believe their husbands—start to mistrust their own inner voice. They wonder if maybe they *are* crazy.

So when the truth about this manipulation comes out, it can rock these women's sense of trust and safety about their own husbands, the men they believed they should have been able to trust implicitly. It's the emotional equivalent of opening a Christmas present full of garbage.

WENDY

Even if you're lucky enough to avoid significant trauma, you still may feel loneliness and isolation. Women in distress about their partner's compulsions feel cut off from their friends and family and society at large, as if they are "living a lie."[8] Compulsive pornography use can be perceived as so illicit and shameful in our culture that these women feel like they have to keep their partner's porn use a secret—that there is no one and nowhere they can turn to for help.

Loneliness can be toxic. Harvard researchers have recently completed a massive seventy-five-year study about well-being, in which they found that close relationships were the strongest predictors of both happiness and longevity—above physical fitness, IQ, and even genetics. What's more, the researchers found that "loneliness kills. It's as powerful as smoking or alcoholism."[9]

And if all that isn't enough, you're also at risk of developing body-image issues and eating disorders as a result of your partner's porn use. Negative body image is already rife for people today without porn exacerbating that. It's another of porn's nasty side effects. Both women who view porn themselves and those whose romantic partners have watched it regularly suffer from eating disorders and negative body image.[10] When interviewed about sex, adolescent girls who knew boys their age were watching porn admitted to doubting their abilities to compete with the women in pornography.[11] Even *men* who watch pornography often suffer from poor body image.[12]

It's the effects of supernormal stimuli again. When you're the real, natural deal, how do you compete with a fantasy? Yes, the women in pornography are real people—you may even call them victims of a predatory industry. But that industry subsists on sucking viewers into an experience that extends far beyond the boundaries of what nature intended.

YOU MAY HAVE TO CONFRONT A COMPULSION

This might be the hardest part of living with a porn consumer. He might not just dabble in porn—his pornography use may have developed into a compulsion that he relies on to cope with life, which may come with a range of side effects.

Why is it so easy for pornography use to turn into a compulsion for a guy? Well, here's at least part of the story: our sex-saturated society is hijacking basic male biology. Have you ever heard someone say, "men are visual," like they're dispensing some wisdom about men that needs no empirical justification? I've heard it, and I used to be skeptical about its origins. Was it just some old wives' tale, like how John Crapper invented the toilet or how we only use ten percent of our brains or how the nursery rhyme "Ring Around the Rosies" is about the Black Plague? If it's even true, what makes men more "visual" than women?

Here's what I found out: the adage that "men are visual" has to do with a difference in our brains. Many studies, most recently a 2018 study in *Neuroimage*,[13] have found that men respond to images of attractive females in their nucleus accumbens, a part of the brain that also lights up when a person sees an object of an addiction, like cocaine. And they process those images in their amygdala, the part of the brain responsible for fear and other emotions. In short, a man has an intense response to a visual image of a person they're attracted to that's both instantaneous and primal. Women, by contrast, experience and process an image of someone they're attracted to in their prefrontal cortex, the part of the brain responsible for language, logic, and executive function.

What's more, after men process those images in their amygdala, over the ensuing days, weeks, or even months or years, those images will continue to pop into their head unbidden. The images can return again and again without intention. This leaves men susceptible to compulsive pornography use. Yes, women can also develop a compulsion to watch porn, but it happens to women less frequently. Studies have found that just three to six percent of women in committed relationships use more pornography than their male partners.[14]

I've brought up the neuroimaging studies that have shown that compulsive porn users' brains respond to porn in the same way that smokers or heroin addicts' brains respond to their drug of choice. Essentially, two things happen when a compulsive porn user watches porn: First, when they're triggered to watch porn, they get a dump of the neurotransmitter dopamine, which makes them crave porn intensely. Second, when they give into their cravings, they get a boost in a different neurotransmitter that makes them (get this) *enjoy it less* than someone who doesn't use porn habitually. Thus, a compulsive porn user wants porn more but *likes* it less once they see it.[15]

This can cause a whole host of problems. The dopamine dump makes it that much harder to abstain from porn when a person is trying to quit. The fact that they start to enjoy it less means their behaviors can sometimes escalate to stranger or more hard-core types of porn or acting out with people online or in the real world to achieve the same level of enjoyment. The shame some men feel about their porn use increases their cravings to use porn in order to cope. And that shame also causes them to lie, hide their behaviors, and experience plenty of mood swings. They often become angry, resentful, emotionally disconnected, and hopeless as they sink further into a porn habit.

And when they try to stop, they have feelings of withdrawal. They get cranky and agitated. They can't focus on anything else. They start to believe they *need* porn to feel normal.

THE GOOD NEWS

Okay, I'm going to take off my Grim Reaper mask for a minute, because even *I'm* feeling a little overwhelmed by the porn monster. It's not all bad news.

A porn history doesn't have to mean your relationship is doomed. Each relationship is unique. And there's a lot of evidence that the effects of porn use are reversible.

Remember the guys with porn-induced erectile dysfunction, the ones whose pornography use rewired their brains so they could no longer have sex with a real person? Of those guys, the ones who gave up porn entirely (or "rebooted," as they like to call it) report that they returned to a healthy sex life within a few months. They also report that the mood fluctuations that come with heavy porn use (e.g., depression, social anxiety, loss of motivation) disappeared along with the porn.

And what about the porn users who lost interest in their partners or were likely to stray? In one study, after just three weeks of giving up porn, previous porn users were found to be as committed to their romantic partners as people who didn't use porn at all.[16]

ADAM

You have a lot of reasons to be optimistic. Yes, as a therapist I have seen the worst of the pain a couple can experience when one member ends up heavily involved with pornography. But I couldn't keep doing what I do if I only saw tragedy, day-in and day-out.

Many people I work with in therapy end up getting better, even if progress is slow. Yes, it can be a long road, but if you want it, you can have it, assuming you're willing to put in the work. From my point of view, when people don't succeed in recovery, it's because they haven't been given the right tools.

So let's wake up from this spooky night of what your marriage could hold and spend the next few chapters learning which tools you need and what conversations you can have to change your future.

JACOB   OCTOBER 2003

Jacob stirs in the low rays of blinding sun through his apartment window, pinned under heavy blankets, disoriented from daytime sleep. Six years and a technological revolution have passed.

Jacob pulls his alarm clock close, squinting. 4:08. *Sigh.* He skipped all three of his classes today, all upper-level engineering ones. His failing grades in two of them mean he'll probably have to add another semester of school to retake those classes. This was not a day to miss any more class. But last night, he watched scene after scene of porn like an amped-up zombie in his locked bedroom while his roommates slept, every hour telling himself that this would be the last video. It was never enough. At dawn, he finally heaved himself into bed, too tired to feel the emptiness, determined to get ninety minutes of sleep and then go to class. But the tentacles of high-speed internet porn have sucked him in too many nights in a row, and at the sound of his alarm, he rolled over and went back to sleep.

He stretches and sits up. His mouth feels dry, his teeth coated in filmy gunk. He closes his eyes to steady his spinning head. And then he reflexively walks over to his door, checks the lock, and sits down at his desk, turning on his laptop. He isn't planning on starting his term paper in World History right now. As the computer boots up, Jacob glances at the calendar on the corkboard above his desk. Thirteen consecutive days filled with red X's. He looks at the six hopeful blank squares before that. Nearly two weeks ago, it looked like he would at last conquer this beast. All he needed were some goals and a calendar. No one would have to know what it was for. And it worked! For six whole days. And now...

Thirteen days of porn use in a row. What is he doing? This *has* to stop. It's killing his grades. Jacob feels like two different people, and he doesn't really like one of them. He can't seem to look any of his peers in the eye, let alone form those lasting college friendships everyone is always going on about. And forget about girls.

That stupid calendar is staring at him. He stands up, tears it off the wall, leaving a ragged corner swaying under the pushpin. He lets the calendar fall to the floor as he sits down. But this time, instead of going straight for the mouse, he lays his head in his hands.

This is such a disaster.

But even as he wallows, one last resort looms in his mind. The one he's been avoiding for years.

Jacob picks up the cordless phone from his nightstand, pauses, then sets it down again. He picks it up again, steeling himself as he dials the first phone number he ever memorized, then holds his breath through three eternal rings. He hears his dad's tinny "hello?" from over five hundred miles away. So many times he's tried to have this conversation since he came to college, always chickening out, confessing instead how much more he struggles in his engineering classes than he thought he would, then asking about Mom and Matt, finally settling on bonding over cars. Each time, he tells himself that he's working up to the big confession that never comes.

But this time, before any chit chat can derail Jacob's nerve, he blurts, "Dad, put Mom on the phone. I need to talk to both of you."

"All right. Hold on."

Some muffled background footsteps, soft voices, and then the crisp "hello?" that's as familiar to him as any voice on earth.

Here goes. "Mom. Dad. I've been watching stuff I shouldn't. I've been watching pornography. I hate that I do it. But I can't stop. I've tried everything. I've really tried." His voice breaks. After all of the tiptoeing around his house, the midnight channel surfing with the volume on mute, in the end it's Jacob who's shouting it from the rooftops.

He waits, listening to the void. How many seconds can he handle? How angry will they be? Or worse, how disappointed?

His mom finally breaks the silence.

"Oh, sweetie. We had no idea. Jeff, can we get him into counseling there? Let's get you into counseling."

"Good idea, Sharon. I'll make some calls. And Jacob— Listen, son, it's gonna be all right."

"Oh. Okay. Yes, thank you!"

And just like that, for the first time in eleven years, the muscles in Jacob's body relax. It's done now. And after everything, it was okay. It's gonna be just fine. He feels heavy, like after all of his sleep, he needs some real rest now. Like he could just melt into the floor and breathe at last.

1   Sun, Chyng, Ana Bridges, Jennifer A. Johnson, and
       Matthew B. Ezzell. "Pornography and the male sexual
       script: An analysis of consumption and sexual relations."
       Archives of Sexual Behavior 45, no. 4 (2016): 983-994.

       Schneider, Jennifer P. "Effects of cybersex addiction
       on the family: Results of a survey." Sexual Addiction &
       Compulsivity: *The Journal of Treatment and Prevention* 7,
       no. 1-2 (2000): 31-58.

       Weinstein, Aviv M., Rinat Zolek, Anna Babkin, Koby
       Cohen, and Michel Lejoyeux. "Factors predicting
       cybersex use and difficulties in forming intimate
       relationships among male and female users of cybersex."
       Frontiers in Psychiatry 6 (2015).

       Harkness, Emily. "Internet pornography: associations
       with sexual risk behaviour, sexual scripts & use within
       relationships." Master's thesis. University of Sydney.
       (2014). ses.library.usyd.edu.au

       Bergner, Raymond M., and Ana J. Bridges. "The
       significance of heavy pornography involvement for
       romantic partners: Research and clinical implications."
       Journal of Sex & Marital Therapy 28, no. 3 (2002): 193-
       206.

       Willoughby, Brian J., Jason S. Carroll, Dean M. Busby,
       and Cameron C. Brown. "Differences in pornography use
       among couples: Associations with satisfaction, stability,
       and relationship processes." *Archives of Sexual Behavior*
       45, no. 1 (2016): 145-158.

2   Schneider, Jennifer P. "Effects of cybersex addiction
       on the family: Results of a survey." *Sexual Addiction &*

Compulsivity: The Journal of Treatment and Prevention 7, no. 1-2 (2000): 31-58.

3   Bridges, Ana J., Robert Wosnitzer, Erica Scharrer, Chyng Sun, and Rachael Liberman. "Aggression and sexual behavior in best-selling pornography videos: A content analysis update." *Violence Against Women* 16, no. 10 (2010): 1065-1085.

4   Sun, Chyng, Ana Bridges, Jennifer A. Johnson, and Matthew B. Ezzell. "Pornography and the male sexual script: An analysis of consumption and sexual relations." *Archives of Sexual Behavior* 45, no. 4 (2016): 983-994.

5   Maddox, Penny M., Galena K. Rhoades, and Howard J. Markman. "Viewing sexually-explicit materials alone or together: Associations with relationship quality." *Archives of Sexual Behavior* 40, no. 2 (2011): 441-448.

6   Lambert, Nathaniel M., Sesen Negash, Tyler F. Stillman, Spencer B. Olmstead, and Frank D. Fincham. "A love that doesn't last: Pornography consumption and weakened commitment to one's romantic partner." *Journal of Social and Clinical Psychology* 31, no. 4 (2012): 410.

7   Steffens, Barbara A., and Robyn L. Rennie. "The traumatic nature of disclosure for wives of sexual addicts." *Sexual Addiction & Compulsivity* 13, no. 2-3 (2006): 247-267.

Bergner, Raymond M., and Ana J. Bridges. "The significance of heavy pornography involvement for romantic partners: Research and clinical implications." *Journal of Sex & Marital Therapy* 28, no. 3 (2002): 193-206.

8   Bergner, Raymond M., and Ana J. Bridges. "The significance of heavy pornography involvement for

romantic partners: Research and clinical implications." *Journal of Sex & Marital Therapy* 28, no. 3 (2002): 193-206.

9   Mineo, Liz. "Good Genes are Nice, but Joy is Better." *The Harvard Gazette*, April 11, 2017. https://news.harvard.edu/gazette/story/2017/04/over-nearly-80-years-harvard-study-has-been-showing-how-to-live-a-healthy-and-happy-life/ (accessed February 13, 2022).

10   Tylka, Tracy L., and Rachel M. Calogero. "Perceptions of male partner pressure to be thin and pornography use: Associations with eating disorder symptomatology in a community sample of adult women." *International Journal of Eating Disorders* (2019).

       Bergner, Raymond M., and Ana J. Bridges. "The significance of heavy pornography involvement for romantic partners: Research and clinical implications." *Journal of Sex & Marital Therapy* 28, no. 3 (2002): 193-206.

       Bridges, Ana, Raymond Bergner, and Matthew Hesson-McInnis. "Romantic partners use of pornography: Its significance for women." *Journal of Sex & Marital Therapy* 29, no. 1 (2003): 1-14.

       Daneback, Kristian, Bente Træen, and Sven-Axel Månsson. "Use of pornography in a random sample of Norwegian heterosexual couples." *Archives of Sexual Behavior* 38, no. 5 (2009): 746-753.

11   Walker, Shelley, Meredith Temple-Smith, Peter Higgs, and Lena Sanci. "'It's always just there in your face': young people's views on porn." *Sexual Health* 12, no. 3 (2015): 200-206.

12   Sun, Chyng, Ana Bridges, Jennifer A. Johnson, and Matthew B. Ezzell. "Pornography and the male sexual script: An analysis of consumption and sexual relations." *Archives of Sexual Behavior* 45, no. 4 (2016): 983-994.

13   Strahler, J., Onno Kruse, S. Wehrum-Osinsky, Tim Klucken, and Rudolf Stark. "Neural correlates of gender differences in distractibility by sexual stimuli." *Neuroimage* 176 (2018): 499-509

14   Willoughby, Brian J., Jason S. Carroll, Dean M. Busby, and Cameron C. Brown. "Differences in pornography use among couples: Associations with satisfaction, stability, and relationship processes." *Archives of Sexual Behavior* 45, no. 1 (2016): 145-158.

        Daneback, Kristian, Bente Træen, and Sven-Axel Månsson. "Use of pornography in a random sample of Norwegian heterosexual couples." *Archives of Sexual Behavior* 38, no. 5 (2009): 746-753.

15   Voon, Valerie, Thomas B. Mole, Paula Banca, Laura Porter, Laurel Morris, Simon Mitchell, Tatyana R. Lapa et al. "Neural correlates of sexual cue reactivity in individuals with and without compulsive sexual behaviours." *PloS one* 9, no. 7 (2014): e102419.

16   Lambert, Nathaniel M., Sesen Negash, Tyler F. Stillman, Spencer B. Olmstead, and Frank D. Fincham. "A love that doesn't last: Pornography consumption and weakened commitment to one's romantic partner." *Journal of Social and Clinical Psychology* 31, no. 4 (2012): 410-438.

PART TWO:

THE TALK

(discussing the problem)

4. TWO QUESTIONS
AND A PARADOX:
ARE YOU READY FOR THE TALK?

I believe in a world where embracing your light doesn't mean ignoring your dark.
—Kevin Breel

WENDY

Remember when you were a kid how having "The Talk" meant that your parents had trapped you somewhere so you could bond through the shared horror of discussing the mechanics of sex? Then when you got older and started dating, you had "The Talk" when you'd reached that point in a relationship when you wanted to date exclusively, so you had to build up the courage to ask, "Sooo... are we boyfriend-girlfriend or what?"

Well, there's a new kind of talk in town. In some ways, it draws on previous iterations of The Talk—some of the awkwardness of addressing human sexuality combined with an opportunity to define where you both stand in your relationship. This version will require you to be brave and upfront. If you want to know how involved someone you're dating has been with pornography, you're going to have to ask him. You're going to have The Talk.

And maybe your parents chickened out of the sex talk with you, and you had to learn everything from kids on the playground or your high school gym teacher's feeble attempt at sex ed. Maybe you've never had the chance to have that special "are we or aren't we?" conversation with a guy. If that's the case, we've got plenty of extra help for you here.

ADAM

Take a deep breath. In these next few chapters, I'm going to guide you through The Talk, minimizing anxiety for both of you. You don't have to execute this conversation perfectly to get it right. It probably will get a little messy, and that's okay.

This chapter is all about timing—identifying the right time in your life and relationship when you'll be ready for this conversation. Chapter Five will teach you the reasons why ordinary people with good intentions sometimes lie and why honesty needs to be your number-one goal regarding The Talk. In Chapter Six, we'll introduce you to The Warm-up Talk, a crucial conversation that will help you prepare your partner for The Talk without blindsiding him. Chapter Seven guides you through the steps of The Talk itself. In Chapter Eight, we'll help you to identify unexpected emotions you may have about The Talk and figure out what to do about them. And the rest of the book will be about working together to conquer a porn habit and build a fantastic marriage.

But before anything else, you'll have to make sure *you* are ready for this conversation. This means you're going to have to answer yes to two questions, the first of which is:

IS NOW THE RIGHT TIME IN OUR RELATIONSHIP TO BRING UP PORNOGRAPHY?

The answer is no if you've just met and you're only having fun together. Maybe you're hanging out, going bowling, whatever. Your date might be a little bit surprised (and not in the "Surprise! Happy Birthday!" way) if you just struck up a conversation about porn between frames at the bowling alley.

What about a blind date? Well, unless you never want your friend to set you up on another blind date again, don't have this conversation on a blind date. No first dates. If you wouldn't decide together on debt reduction strategies or whether you want to name your firstborn son Aiden, Kaden, or Jaden on a first date, don't bring up porn. No second dates or group dates, either. It would be pretty awkward if you attempted The Talk around six other people.

Now, you might *want* to talk about porn on the first date. I've known a number of women who have. But The Talk just won't work when you're making small talk and getting to know each other, deciding whether you can trust one another. Neither of you can reasonably expect raw honesty about private matters yet.

This is the conversation you'll have when your relationship gets serious: when you're talking marriage or long-term commitment, after you've said the "L" word, certainly by the time you're engaged. Let's reserve this conversation for when you're starting to plan a future together.

I think there are two reasons some women ask their dates about porn too soon. The first is a fear of investing in a relationship where she might get hurt. She's afraid of getting close to someone, finding out later that he has an extensive history of porn use that will complicate her marriage, and then having her heart broken when things fall apart.

The problem is, there's no insurance against heartbreak. Even in good, healthy marriages, people get hurt from time to time. You always put yourself at risk when you love another human being. We humans are funny creatures—we can't live without one another, and so we risk a lot of pain to have love in our lives.

And other women bring up porn too early because they're hoping to get it out of the way, as if it's just a perfunctory item on the dating game checklist: What's his major? (Check.) Is he good with children? (Check.) No criminal record? (Check.) And what about pornography? (Check.)

The problem with the checklist mentality is that The Talk isn't the kind of conversation you get out of the way. You confront a history of pornography use together. This won't be a one-off conversation that you lock away in a box and never speak of again. Even if the guy you date has seen very little porn, if you have kids someday, you'll have to address pornography with them down the road when they come across it.

So if you're in the right place in your relationship for The Talk, you'll still have to answer yes to this second question:

AM I READY TO HEAR HIS ANSWERS?

If you're expecting a *specific* answer, then you're not ready to ask the questions. Maybe you can't handle the possibility that he's struggled with pornography use. Maybe you're okay with a history of porn use, but you need it to be in the past. Maybe you've already decided that you need him to admit that he's addicted to porn, so that you can jump in and fix the problem right away.

Whenever we decide that we need a certain outcome, we set ourselves up for disappointment. Conversations never go exactly how we want them to. So wait to have The Talk until you care enough about him as a person that you're open to hearing whatever he has to say.

But what if talking about pornography is an intense emotional experience for you? Maybe porn has affected your life in a negative way, and you're still working through your emotions about it. Maybe you've already dated or been married to a pornography user, and it's painful to imagine going through anything similar. Maybe the idea of porn just makes you sick to your stomach, and you don't even know why.

The Talk needs to feel safe for both of you. If you need a little more time to emotionally prepare, then take it. We'll talk in Chapter Eight about how your emotions are powerful messengers, how to understand where they're coming from, as well as how to express those feelings.

WENDY

The fact is, there's very little chance that the guy you're dating hasn't at least seen or even experimented with pornography in this day and age. And that might be difficult to hear, since from the time we were little girls, we've been fed this mythos of The Perfect Guy. You know what I'm talking about.

Maybe some well-meaning soul once advised you to write down your "perfect husband" list. At a church meeting when I was sixteen, I wrote my exhaustive list of everything I wanted my true love to be, my marriage manifesto etched in glitter pen. I don't have mine anymore, but the list usually looks something like this:

MR. RIGHT: THE SHORT LIST

1. Must be a doppelganger for the guy who plays Thor
2. Has both a British and an Australian accent at the same time
3. Can play Chopin on the piano better than Chopin himself
4. Is fluent in Spanish, French, Mandarin, as well as Ancient and Modern Greek
5. Works as a world-renowned neurosurgeon *and* astrophysicist
6. Is independently wealthy
7. Somehow became independently wealthy by curing orphans' malaria in Doctors without Borders
8. Solved cold fusion
9. Is good with kids
10. Has the impeccable manners and dreamy broodiness of Mr. Darcy, the spiritual wisdom of the Dalai Lama, and the all-American attitude (and perfect hair) (and abs) of Superman
11. Is hopelessly, single-mindedly, unerringly devoted to me

So that's maybe an exaggeration of the list. But not by much. And on the one hand, you should give some real thought to the core qualities you want in a partner because you do want to keep your eyes wide open before marriage. You know it isn't in your best interest to run away with the first deadbeat rando who looks your way.

But on the other hand, sometimes all that dreaming and planning can lead to unrealistic expectations about your life partner. Like you, he probably fought with his siblings growing up and went through that pimple-faced, ugly-duckling stage in junior high. He's probably done a thing or two that he's not proud of during the messiness of life. I bet you have too. And he probably just wants to love and be loved in spite of all of that.

Marrying somebody real—amazing and wonderful and *real*—will be so much more rewarding than searching for a flawless knight in shining armor with a perfect jawline who doesn't exist.

When Cinderella's coach turned to pumpkins and her magical night evaporated, her dreams were put on hold. Likewise, all marriages have their pumpkins-at-midnight moments. They aren't always pornography. They might be depression, mental and physical illness, significant financial struggles, loss, grief, infertility, intense disagreement and personality differences, crises of faith, or any other catastrophe. Some of these hardships can take years and a good deal of heartbreak to overcome. They definitely require the commitment of both partners to put each other first and see things through.

But the pumpkins-at-midnight times are also an opportunity to develop a deep and grounded love for each other, one more beautiful than infatuation and fairy tales. It's the kind of love American icon of kindness Mr. Fred Rogers describes when he says, "Love isn't a state of perfect caring. It is an active noun like 'struggle.' To love someone is to strive to accept that person exactly the way he or she is, right here and now—and to go on caring even through times that may bring us pain."[1]

EMBRACE THE PARADOX

ADAM

A paradox is an interesting thing. It occurs when two opposing elements coexist in one entity, but it somehow all works together, almost like magic. Take, for example, Jesus' paradoxical wisdom, "Be wise as serpents, but harmless as doves." Or the way the late great boxer Muhammad Ali described the paradox of boxing: "Float like a butterfly, sting like a bee."

Throughout The Talk and beyond, I'll ask you to behave in ways that may seem contradictory: compassionate and understanding, but firm in your resolve. You'll need to ask direct questions but not interrogate your partner. You'll learn you're not responsible for his well-being, but at the same time you won't want to be distant and heartless. You'll both need to be vulnerable while understanding there are no guarantees you won't get hurt.

You probably default to one of these two approaches. Maybe you lean toward an assertive, take-no-prisoners attitude. Or maybe you're a keep-the-peace, don't-rock-the-boat kind of person. People tend to lean one way or the other in most of life's interactions.

The key is, don't give up the qualities that come naturally to you. But do stretch yourself; spend some time out of your comfort zone. If you're a strong-willed, feisty warrior princess, work on empathy. And if you're the forgiving, accepting type, focus on voicing your own needs. Embracing this paradox gives you flexibility. And in every single marital interaction, flexibility is one of your greatest assets, because the more flexible you are, the harder it is for you to snap.

There's a place for the range of human characteristics in life. There will be times when you'll need to stick up for yourself. At other times, a situation will call for selfless compassion. And I'm telling you to choose all of it. Wear both hats. Embrace the paradox.

Once you're at the point in your relationship when you're ready to discuss pornography and you've begun to embrace the paradox, it's time to build honesty into the process.

JACOB   NOVEMBER 2003

Bent over his desk, charcoal pencil in hand, his engineering notebook pushed off to the side, Jacob shades the angular image of a man in a fedora and trenchcoat standing under the bare branches of a tree. The top third of the page is empty, waiting for the perfect title that hasn't yet struck.

Jacob half-listens to his engineering professor drone on about field-programmable gated arrays while he designs the marquee poster for when his hard-boiled mystery makes it to the silver screen. But even as he tries to focus on the lecture, Jacob envisions mysterious disappearances. Clues and red herrings. The brilliant but troubled detective Mark Lexington. Tragic Clarisse de la Troix who will fall madly for Mark just before the ending. He has to get this right.

As the bell rings, Jacob yawns and stretches, widening his droopy eyes, and packs up to head home for a couple of hours. He stayed out with Steve and Laura until 2 AM last night, laughing over milkshakes, then hitting the bowling alley where the insomniac students spend the witching hour. He sat next to Laura on the plastic chairs as Steve was up to bowl, hoping that Steve and Laura didn't have any romance brewing. Jacob almost told her about his novel. He wondered if she'd laugh at him. But who knows? Maybe she'd lean in closer and ask him more about it.

Jacob is surprised by how much his therapist—a soft-spoken, bespectacled man not much older than Jacob—has helped him out. He gives Jacob advice about how to distract himself from porn by working on his novel and putting himself out there with friends.

Hanging out in the front room of his apartment with Steve was easier than Jacob thought it would be. Steve doesn't seem to mind doing all the talking when the subject turns to sports (as it usually does) or the fact that he and Jacob wouldn't have broken the jock-nerd barrier in high school. And Steve has started asking Jacob to join them whenever Laura stops by to hang out. Jacob sometimes imagines asking Laura out, just the two of them. But would she even say yes? When Jacob is with Laura, she listens like everything he says is the most interesting thing she's heard.

Jacob's dad acts as his new sobriety calendar. Every day Jacob sends his dad an email with just one number in the subject line. Typing "30" yesterday made Jacob sit a little taller. Thirty days porn-free feels miles ahead of twenty-nine.

Jacob rushes through the door of his apartment and heads straight for his room. He should probably get some ramen in him, since this is his only chance to eat before this evening. But Jacob only has thoughts of his novel.

He hasn't missed a single class in four weeks, so these writing hours are sacrosanct. Some days he stares at the blank computer screen for the better part of an hour. Or trance-like, he types two thousand or more words in one stretch, only to delete most of them the next day.

When he sits down at his computer and boots it up, he rubs his hands together, planning the scene where Mark and Clarisse first meet. As he notices the flashing red light on his cordless phone, he picks it up and dials his voicemail. The computerized female voice alerts him that a message from his mom is waiting for him. Jacob's heart thumps. She worries too much, treats Jacob like a delicate object that might shatter if mishandled. Jacob never knows how to say, "I'm okay, Mom." Last week he snapped at her with a terse, "I'm fine!" just to stop the questions.

Jacob sets the phone down, ignoring the voicemail. It's time to figure out Clarisse for the next scene. But how do you write the perfect woman and make her seem real at the same time? What will Mark do to get Clarisse's attention?

He opens the web browser and searches for some classic leading ladies from Old Hollywood for inspiration and clicks on the first result. On a site about starlets of the Golden Age, he's immediately bombarded with photos more alluring than he planned on, images that ignite something in him. Something he's been fighting to suppress. More times than Jacob can count over the past weeks, he's resisted the urge to look, done something else, gone out bowling, planned his novel.

This time he walks over to his door, locks it, and slides right back to the Jacob of thirty days ago. A few searches and clicks later, he's left glamorous old Hollywood and entered the darker alleyways of the internet.

Only an hour later, his mind clears for a moment and he remembers. He remembers his parents' sacrifices to pay for the counseling that's meant to be his salvation. He recalls the emails to his dad, more promising with each passing day. He thinks of the years he felt like he'd never overcome this, never be normal. He closes the site, tapping the mouse harder than he needs to.

And then he sees it at the top of his open email. An unread message from his dad with a single question mark in the subject line. Of course. He hasn't sent his dad his email yet today. His face drains its color. He owes it to Mom and Dad to beat this thing.

He closes his eyes and furrows his brow. Okay, okay. This was a mistake, a blip. It was a learning experience that he won't repeat. It was good, really, to see how easily a mistake can happen. He can keep up his momentum, starting immediately.

And he doesn't want to worry anybody.

He presses "reply" on the email, deletes the question mark from the subject line, types "31" and hits "send."

1 Rogers, Fred. *The World According to Mr. Rogers: Important Things to Remember*. Westport: Hyperion, 2003.

5. THE IMPORTANCE
OF BEING HONEST

The truth will set you free.
—Jesus

ADAM

Not to incriminate myself, but here we go: In elementary school my brother and I were in a goofy feud with a neighbor girl. I don't know why. I think it started when she told us our skateboard moves were stupid.

One fine, California summer day, my brother and I were eating microwaved frozen burritos (lunch of champions) in our front yard when it suddenly occurred to my brother to squander the last half of his burrito by tossing it onto this girl's roof. It seemed like a decent idea at the time (hint: it wasn't). Even though my timid brother has never been known for his pitching arm, he somehow swung that burrito high in the sky, right onto Amanda's roof with as much bravado as I ever saw him display. It was glorious.

But shortly after that, it became a well-known fact around the neighborhood that my brother threw the burrito and I passively allowed it to happen (I *might* have encouraged it). My dad was not happy with either of us. We each had to sit in "the chair" for an entire hour, just staring at the wall—the largest chair-time punishment ever handed out for a single incident in the history of the family.

A week or two later, Amanda confronted us about the burrito incident. She knew we did it. We knew she knew we did it. But we weren't expecting her to come right out and ask us about it. So we both lied. We told her it wasn't us. All three of us knew it was us. But we denied it anyway. As you'll find out in this chapter, people often lie when they're ambushed and don't have time to make a sound decision, *even* when lying doesn't make any sense.

WHY PEOPLE LIE

WENDY

The hard truth: if you blindside your boyfriend with The Talk, he may lie about his pornography use. As Adam said, people lie. It's not a "guy" thing. It's not a "jerk" thing. It's not a "complete lack of moral compass" thing. It's a human thing. Even people who take pride in their integrity are shocked to find themselves lying in the moment sometimes. More often than not, lying is about self-preservation, and we're biologically wired for self-preservation.

Take kids, for example: We praise small children for their authenticity, their creativity, their confidence and optimism, their acceptance of others, etc. As adults, it would be nice to have some of those childlike attributes again. Kids are also basically professional liars.

Lying starts young. One-fifth of children are lying at around two years of age, not long after language develops. By age four, ninety percent of kids are lying.[1] As soon as they could talk, my kids used to lie whenever they had a messy diaper, hoping I'd ignore the stench so they could keep on playing. Years ago, my newly potty-trained daughter once told me her baby brother had pooped her underpants that *she was still wearing*. (Although kids lie intuitively, they don't always tell the most *believable* whoppers.)

For most kids, lying starts to drop off at about twelve years of age.[2] The majority of children grow up into adults who believe in being truthful and who expect honesty from others in return. But as Adam illustrated with his fantastic flying burrito and the pointless subterfuge afterward, sometimes people lie when they're caught off guard. Depending on the family culture your partner comes from, when you surprise him by asking about his porn use, he may worry that disclosing everything means losing you, and he'll revert to being that little kid who lies when he's blindsided. He may not have been planning on revealing that information right then and there, so he needs time to prepare.

A tall, lanky guy with floppy hair that hangs over one eye, Edwin is only the second man I spoke to about his experience with porn. Gentle and soft-spoken, he lights up when he talks about his enthusiasm for reading, particularly the great fantasy stories like *Harry Potter* and *The Lord of the Rings*. He's in his mid-thirties, single, and you don't have to talk to him for long before you learn how much people matter to him. He describes his sister, nine years his junior, as if she is his best friend. He looks forward to the time they spend together and cares about her opinion of him.

Edwin is also a compulsive pornography user. He shares the details of his porn use with me, but he doesn't seem proud of it. Sometimes, embarrassed, he hides his face in his hands. He tells me everything anyway. I'm often surprised by his frankness. He says he's learned to be totally honest.

He wasn't always transparent about his porn habit. About eighteen months earlier, he was dating a girl, Shawna. She seemed to be The One. At one point Shawna told Edwin they needed to talk. She needed to be sure of something. She listed for him all of her "dealbreakers" in a relationship. Between "no felonies" and "no history of violence," she rattled off "no porn." "None of those things are an issue for you, right?" she asked. Edwin gulped out a "no," even though he knew it wasn't true. He didn't know why he just couldn't quit watching porn, when he preferred Shawna to anything on a lifeless screen. He resolved to just stop the porn, right then and there. *Then,* he thought, *maybe I'm not really lying.*

It didn't work. Edwin couldn't understand why. He loved Shawna and wanted to be with her. Their relationship progressed, so he bought a ring and proposed, all while he was watching porn every day. The guilt was eating away at him. He wished he had just been honest with Shawna from the get-go. He had to tell her.

They'd been engaged for about two weeks when he got up the gumption to pull her aside with his own "we need to talk" speech. They went for a walk. With all the courage he could muster, he told her about the porn. "I've been struggling with a porn addiction for a long time now. I'm trying everything to give it up." He told me her face just went white before he pleaded, "I promise I'll figure out how to quit!"

She just left.

Over the next days and months, Edwin called and texted her. She never responded. Maybe she'd been abducted by aliens. Maybe she was on the lam for a secret bank heist from a double life she lived. But Edwin was pretty sure the porn use (and his lies about it) had scared her off. His fiancée had just disappeared one day, like a desert mirage when you get too close.

As I said, if you were to meet Edwin, you would be astonished by his honesty. So why did he lie when it mattered most to tell the truth? In order to understand this, we need to talk about dice in a cup.[3]

DICE AND TRUTH TELLING

In 2012 two psychologists recruited seventy-four university students to roll some dice in a cup. Each participant received a six-sided die under a paper cup with a hole in the top. They had to roll the die once, look through the hole, and report the number they rolled. Simple, right? But here's the catch: Students were told they would receive pay based on the number they rolled—the higher the number, the greater the pay. So naturally, students wanted to roll a high number. Or *report* a high number, at least. The researchers had no way of knowing which number each subject rolled.

The students were divided into two equal groups: One group had to disclose their number within eight seconds. The second group could take as much time as they needed to report their number. Then the researchers compared the results with the statistical likelihood of rolling each number to see how much dishonesty was going on.

What the researchers found: The students who were under a time crunch were *significantly* more likely to lie about the number they rolled than the students who could take all the time they needed to decide on their response. In fact, no lying whatsoever was detected among the students who were allowed the time to think over their answer—to ignore their impulses and decide to just be honest. One of the researchers, Dr. Shalvi, concluded, "Although our results reveal a dark side of human tendencies, they also suggest a bright prospect... People can behave in an ethical way—they just need time."[4]

Edwin didn't have any time to consider his response. That's why he lied. If you want to maximize the chance that your future husband will tell you the truth, give him time to prepare.

MEN NEED TIME TO PROCESS

Aside from the human propensity for dishonesty when taken by surprise, your typical male may need more time to process information before having a difficult conversation about it. To write her book, *For Women Only: What You Need to Know About the Inner Lives of Men*, self-help author Shaunti Feldhahn sent out thousands of anonymous questionnaires to men for their feedback on how they really feel about matters relating to the opposite sex. Among many other little-known revelations about men, she found that men tend to be internal processors, which means that they often address issues by pulling away so they can think about them:

> Men can think and talk about baseball, politics, cooking dinner, fixing the deck with no time delay. But on issues of emotional importance,

most men simply need time and space for internal processing. And that may mean a few hours, or for the really big issues, a few days.[5]

Supporting this point, gender researcher Michael Gurian has found that men can take up to seven *hours* longer than women to process complex emotive data.[6]

Although it's becoming increasingly apparent that gender traits are on a spectrum and individual men and women have a range of characteristics that may not be stereotypical of their sex, according to Feldhahn's surveys, most men report that they don't immediately know how to approach an emotionally sensitive topic in a relationship. It's not that they don't care; it's that they need extra time to identify and process their feelings about it. So with something as sensitive as pornography use, where your partner may feel emotions ranging from shame to fear to mortal dread, give him some extra time to think his feelings and experience through and be ready to talk.

GENEVIEVE   JANUARY 2006

Genevieve taps her manicured fingernails on her wrist and stares into space. Why did she agree to come to this house party where she doesn't know anyone but Tyler, who's a decent enough brother, but a terrible wingman? If she meets one more idiot here who drones on and on about his Ford F-150 without bothering to ask her name and looks her body up and down like she doesn't have a face, she will rip Tyler off the ditz he came here for and drag him home by the ear.

As her lion starts to rise, she tries to focus on a blank space of white wall. Breathe in, breathe out. Her chest feels tight. She squeezes her eyes closed, but she can't drown out the crowd or the music.

But then she hears him before she sees him, although what he's saying, she can't be sure. She can only make out the faintest rumble of words over the pounding electronic dance music. He comes into focus on the other side of the tiny front room, tall and curly haired. He's smiling at her.

"WHAT?" she yells.

He seems to consider something and then walks to the stereo in the corner of the room, adjusting the volume to a civilized level. Genevieve's head clears and her heart relaxes. *My freaking hero.*

"What did you think of that test on Thursday?" he repeats, audible now.

Genevieve squints. "Wait— what test?"

"In Stats."

He sits down on a dining chair next to the stereo, fifteen feet away from Genevieve, looking at the wall above her head. "You're in Dr. Boone's class, right?"

"How do you... ?" Genevieve still has to half-shout over two groups of people having their own conversations between them. Genevieve gets up from the threadbare couch and moves to a mismatched one right next to Mystery Man. He sits taller, smiling.

"Are you in Dr. Boone's class? 5:00 PM?"

He nods. "I'm pretty sure I sit a few rows behind you."

"That test was ROUGH!"

"I know, man!" He brushes his hair out of his face. "I expected him to test us on the book. Or at least his lectures. But those questions were out of left field."

"Exactly! I kept hoping it would get better. But no."

"It was really just an educated guessing game. Emphasis on 'guessing,' not 'educated.'"

Genevieve laughs. "Totally. Why are you taking Stats?"

Mystery Man smiles, his eyes meeting hers for the first time. "I'm EE. Electrical Engineering. It's a requirement, but I put it off 'til my last semester."

Hmmm. Not a moron. In fact, this tall, dark stranger in a Led Zeppelin t-shirt doesn't seem to resemble the Neanderthal automatons at this party at all.

"That's really cool! My brother—Tyler—he's over there. The twitterpated one." Genevieve rolls her eyes when she sees Tyler's hands on the waist of a giggly girl, all twirly hair and lips. "He's thinking of studying civil engineering."

"Oh. Well, that's also a major."

Genevieve laughs. "Okay, maybe they're not that similar."

He's still laughing at his own joke. "It's cool. Engineering is engineering. We're snobs over in electrical. Hey, I'm Jacob, by the way."

"I'm Genevieve."

Jacob nods. "That's French."

"It's cool that you know that! My parents were going to pronounce it the French way, Zhon-viev, until they remembered that kids have no mercy. They love Paris. My whole family does. Not that I could ever go." Genevieve's face falls.

"Hey, if you want something bad enough, you can figure it out."

"I'd be happy just figuring out how to get a college degree."

Jacob furrows his brow and looks at Genevieve quizzically.

She sighs. "I'm not actually enrolled at Cedarville. I can only take night classes that aren't already full. Boone added me to Stats out of the goodness of his heart. I want to get as many credits as I can. I still live at home with my parents."

He nods. "Oh. Is that, like, a *bad* thing? Living at home's cool."

"No. Well, I mean— Kind of? It's a long story."

"Tell me, and I'll let you know if it gets boring." Jacob smiles.

"I, umm, I got into the University of Oklahoma a few years ago. I had saved up the cash to pay my way there. My family— They can't put me through college. I'm only at this party because Tyler insists on us having a *real college experience*."

"Yeah, this party is... something else."

Like clockwork, a guy with frosted blonde hair and a chain hanging from his jeans pocket walks past, extending a fist toward Jacob. Jacob hesitates, then fistbumps the guy back. Jacob shrugs his shoulders at Genevieve.

"Do you even know that guy?" Genevieve laughs.

"No." Jacob looks Genevieve in the eye and snickers. "But you were saying..."

"Yeah. So... The summer before I was supposed to leave, my dad took all of my money to buy a car."

His eyes widen. "To buy a car?"

"Yeah. It's... My family's really complicated."

"Sounds like it."

Genevieve sighs."Yeah. So I went to Clark State Community instead. I got my associate's last spring. I've got transfer applications in at some other schools. They're all... far from here. I should get letters soon, one way or another. And I have enough saved up. Again. Don't look at me like that—my dad's not on my account anymore!"

Jacob laughs. "Man, I didn't know some people have to protect themselves from their own parents."

"Yeah. It's... yeah."

"And then what? What's your big dream?" He looks down at his folded hands balanced on his knees.

"I'd love to study marketing."

He raises his eyebrows without looking up. "Really? "

Genevieve flushes. "Well, I like observing what works with sales. The psychology of what makes people *want* something. And *buy* something. I like getting inside people's heads."

"That's cool! Sometimes I wish I had studied journalism, which is almost the same thing."

Genevieve laughs. "Umm, no it isn't. They're nothing alike! Less in common than EE and civil engineering."

"Ha! Yeah, I just... I like figuring out people too. I don't get to do that much with my degree."

Where was this guy those wasted years when Genevieve was dating Brad? "Well, EE is the future. You'll probably design some cool stuff that changes the world." Genevieve hesitates for a second then blurts, "We should team up. I'll sell whatever cutting-edge wizardry you invent."

Jacob chuckles.

Oh, gosh, was that a polite laugh or a genuine one? Genevieve cringes. She'd suddenly love nothing more than to sink into the floor and disappear.

But Jacob looks up and smiles at her again. "We'd be the dream team."

He hesitates. "You know what?"

"What?" She wishes she could stop her voice from fluttering. And she hopes her smile looks less plastered than it feels.

"I bet you can sell anything. I'm going to make you the CEO of my venture." He winks at her.

A thrill passes through Genevieve. She takes off her coat, forgetting about the drafty house. But then she blurts, "Hey, did you drive here?"

"I did." Jacob sits back and crosses his arms, looking at her with a grin. He's going to make her come out and ask it.

Genevieve runs through the drill in her head. Never leave with someone you hardly know. Don't ride alone in a car with a stranger. Don't be too forward with boys. But she feels bold and giddy, as if a door has opened and she can breathe fresh air.

She opens her mouth, and then Tyler is somehow standing right in front of her with the ditz on his arm. "Gen, we gotta go. Dad just called. Apparently he needs help with some project right this minute." Tyler rolls his eyes.

Genevieve's heart sinks. She looks over at Jacob, who's digging at something invisible on the ground with his toe. "Jacob, it was so nice meeting you. I guess I have to go."

Jacob looks up. "Yeah, it's much better than staring at the back of your head in class."

He smiles in a way that makes Genevieve think he means it.

She smiles back. "Well, I... I guess I will see you on Thursday, then."

His face brightens. "On Thursday?"

"In Stats."

"Oh, yeah! See you in Stats!"

Genevieve waves at Jacob as she follows Tyler and his giggly friend out into the night.

1   Lee, Kang. "Little Liars: Development of Verbal Deception in Children." *Child Development Perspectives* 7, no. 2 (2013): 91-96.

2   Lee, Kang. "Little Liars: Development of Verbal Deception in Children." *Child Development Perspectives* 7, no. 2 (2013): 91-96.

3   Shalvi, Shaul, Ori Eldar, and Yoella Bereby-Meyer. "Honesty Requires Time (and Lack of Justifications)." *Psychological Science* 23, no. 10 (2012): 1264-1270.

4   Shalvi, Shaul, Ori Eldar, and Yoella Bereby-Meyer. "Honesty Requires Time (and Lack of Justifications)." *Psychological Science* 23, no. 10 (2012): 1270.

5   Shaunti Feldhahn Feldhahn, Shaunti. *For Women Only: What You Need to Know About the Inner Lives of Men.* Colorado Springs: Multnomah Publishers, 2004.

6   Gurian, Michael. *What Could He Be Thinking? How a Man's Mind Really Works.* New York City: St. Martin's Griffin, 2004.

6. THE WARM-UP

Measure twice, cut once.
—carpenter's proverb

ADAM

Remember the dice in a cup? And the extra seven hours guys need to process emotionally significant information before they can discuss it? Giving your partner time to prepare to be honest will be a gift to both of you. A few days before you have The Talk, you'll prepare him with a brief warm-up talk. This conversation will most likely be short, maybe only a couple of minutes.

Sometimes a couple of minutes makes all the difference. Abraham Lincoln's Gettysburg Address was only two minutes long. If you had to excuse yourself to use the restroom during the address, you would have missed the whole thing. But those two minutes make up one of the most famous speeches in U.S. history. Mere minutes can pack a fierce punch when each precious second is used wisely.

The ideal time for this brief warm-up talk will be at the end of a date or some other activity, sometime when you're about to say goodbye to each other. That way your partner can take time to process what you've told him, and you won't have to pretend to shoot the breeze and avoid the hulking elephant in the room.

During these vital minutes, you'll cover three topics:

1. Your elevator pitch about porn
2. Your desire to sit down with him in the near future to discuss his history with pornography
3. A statement about how crucial honesty is to you

YOUR ELEVATOR PITCH

An *elevator pitch* will help you verbalize your stance on pornography. Entrepreneurs attract investors by delivering an elevator pitch about their business concept. They figure out how to explain their core idea in the time it would take to ride an elevator from one floor of a building to another—because sometimes that's all the time they get with a potential investor. This type of short, direct pitch can also help someone in your personal life see your point of view. Develop an elevator pitch about your feelings on porn. Think about what you want to convey.

You can discuss the dangers of pornography in a dignified, respectful way that makes others pay close attention. Help your future husband understand that a life with you will be so much better than living with some flimsy cardboard butterflies. You deserve more than that.

Here's a sample elevator pitch to get you started:

> I don't want pornography to be a part of my marriage. Porn doesn't teach people anything healthy or real about sex. It warps people's beliefs about human relationships. Porn can become a habit that takes over a person's life. And it objectifies people—especially women. I want to marry someone who understands how I feel about pornography, who feels the same way I do, and

who is committed to keeping it out of our lives.

You could recite that pitch riding from the third to the ninth floor of a high-rise. It's short, to the point, and easy to understand. Take some time to write out your own elevator pitch, and know it well enough that you can explain it anytime, to anyone.

If you're feeling nervous about your pitch (and that's entirely normal), practice delivering it ahead of time—in your head, in the mirror, however you want—but don't stress about saying it perfectly. What matters is getting the ideas across.

PREPARE HIM FOR THE TALK

After beginning your warm-up talk with your elevator pitch, express your need to talk with your partner about his past exposure to porn. And communicate that you want to give him time to prepare to discuss it. You want him to be present and honest for this.

Give him a day or two to be ready to be honest about his history with pornography, but don't leave The Talk for more than a few days, or it will be just looming out there, stressing you out, and you may lose your gumption.

If you already know that the person you're dating is struggling with porn use, he still needs time to prepare for a structured, in-depth conversation about it. He may think that simply having told you a problem exists was enough and that this is a demon he needs to protect you from. He still might not be ready to be transparent with you. Or he might not understand the level of raw honesty you two will need to deal with this together.

If he seems gung-ho to have The Talk right then and there, this might be the sign that you two are open and comfortable with each other, or that he's undaunted by The Talk. But there's also the chance that his knee-jerk reaction to you bringing up porn is to immediately minimize the role it's played in his life.

Let's believe the research here. Even if he *wants* to discuss porn right then, ask him to take some time to think about it anyway. You'll maximize the likelihood he'll be honest with you.

EMPHASIZE HONESTY

This third step is vital. He needs to know that his porn history isn't nearly as important to you as his honesty about it. You want to help him understand that secrets will damage your relationship more than any porn he's seen.

And honesty should be a primary goal you both share. One study found that among couples in which one or both members used pornography, honesty about porn use meant both parties were significantly happier in their relationships than couples in which one party was lying.[1]

WENDY

My husband and I have put this warm-up concept to the test in our own family. Different relationship, different subject matter, but the principle works. I've got an eleven-year-old who is the most affectionate, tender-hearted boy. He is also So. Much. Trouble. Rhyn possesses this perfect cocktail of energy, curiosity, and an appetite for destruction that has catapulted our child-rearing skills to a whole new level.

A few years ago, Rhyn somehow managed to remove his roller blind from his bedroom window and use it as a battering ram to punch a hole in a wall of our brand-new house. When I discovered the waist-high hole the exact size and shape of the end of the blind lying on the floor next to it, I confronted Rhyn about it. He was tight-lipped, feigning oblivion.

So my husband decided to give Rhyn time to choose to tell the truth. He emphasized how much more we care about Rhyn's honesty than what he did wrong, and he asked Rhyn to come tell us what had happened when he was ready. Sure enough, a couple of hours later, Rhyn's little face appeared at our bedroom doorway, white as a sheet but ready to confess that yes, he had single-handedly devalued our real estate investment.

And a couple of weeks later, Rhyn came to me with a tear-stained face, asking sheepishly, "Mom, if I tell you the truth right away, will I not get in trouble?"

I said I couldn't promise there wouldn't be any consequences, but things would go much better if he told the truth. So he relayed how he was throwing batteries at our TV (like I said—So. Much. Trouble.) when "a rainbow line" appeared on the screen and wouldn't go away.

Believe it or not, I was proud of him that day. Rhyn telling the truth didn't magically repair our TV or the hole in our wall, but we'll take our parenting wins when we can get them, and deciding to override his impulse to lie was a big one for him.

ADAM

It's pretty rare, but some guys might outright refuse to talk about pornography or their history with it. If the guy you're dating avoids the topic entirely and won't make space to discuss it, that might be a big red flag—and you'll need to decide if that's a deal-breaker for your relationship.

In a strong marriage, truth is king. I cannot count the number of times a heartbroken wife in my office has confided in me that it's not so much the porn use but the attendant lying that is killing her relationship. Discovering that someone you trust is being dishonest can upend your sense of safety. So this warm-up talk must drive the point home that you value honesty over any perfect illusion he might want to hide behind. Honesty will be your mantra and your battle cry throughout this entire process. I'm not exaggerating—I want you to beat this honesty horse *to death*.

You need to let him know that when he confides in you, you feel close to him. And he has to know that telling a rose-colored, twisted version of the truth doesn't count. He can't *protect* you with lies or half-truths. Sometimes people convince themselves they're being noble when they're not completely honest. That's hugely problematic in my line of work. One of the most common forms of denial that I see in married guys who lie about using porn sounds like this: "I can't tell my wife that I'm involved in pornography again because she's going to be devastated, and it's my job to protect her. So I'm actually doing her a service by *not* telling her." And that's a terrible lie. It's self-protection disguised as altruism.

So give him the time he needs to prepare to be honest, the time to do what's best for your relationship long-term. If he tells the truth, it will make everything that happens afterward easier.

SAMPLE WARM-UP TALK

Here's an example of how this talk might play out. Your individual conversation will of course be unique to your personalities. But this should at least give you fodder to get started.

> You: Hey, before I go, I wanted to ask you something.
> Him: Sure. Is everything okay? Did something bad happen?
> You: No, things are great. The more we're together, the more I never want it to end.
> Him: Same. So what's up?
> You: [Elevator pitch] So it's important to me to discuss difficult topics before we get married. For example, pornography. I know couples whose relationships didn't work out because one partner couldn't stop watching porn and never got help. It's really sad to watch. [Introduce The Talk] I'd like to talk with you about pornography sometime later this week. Basically, I want to make sure porn isn't something that causes us problems someday. And I know it's everywhere, so I want to talk about how we each feel about it, what our experience is with it, and whether we need to do something to work on overcoming it.
> Him: Yeah, that's understandable. It's not an issue for me, so we should be fine.
> You: [Emphasis on honesty] That's great, but I want to take some time to think about it first. Honesty matters to me more than anything else in our relationship. Even if you had a long history of porn use, I'd rather know up front than just pretend everything regarding pornography is fine, when it's not.

Him: Yeah, I get that. I really haven't looked at it that much. A little back when I was a teenager. But it's in the past.

You: If it's okay with you, can we both take a couple days and think carefully before we talk about it? I'll tell you about my own exposure to porn as well. I want to do this right and would rather slow down and take some time. It would mean a lot to me. Your honesty would really help me trust you—even more than I do now. Can we plan some time in a couple days to just talk? I don't want it to be awkward. I just care about this issue a lot, and I don't want to rush through it. Can we do that?

Him: Totally. That's fine. Maybe we can get some food Friday and talk about whatever you want.

You: Thank you! I really appreciate this.

GENEVIEVE   FEBRUARY 2006

Dr. Boone thrusts his index finger in the air, trying his best to spark some enthusiasm for stats in any of the hundred or so students in the class. Genevieve isn't sure it's working.

"So you see, multiple regression and multivariate regression are *not* the same thing at all!"

Jacob leans over and asks, "So when are we gonna make our plan for world domination?" in a low whisper only Genevieve can hear.

Suddenly bold, Genevieve leans over and whispers, "Umm, how about now? You could come over to my house. We could make spaghetti. I don't have anything until work tomorrow morning."

The hair on the back of Genevieve's neck stands enthusiastically on end. Sitting next to Jacob the past three weeks has made stats exciting, although not for the reasons Dr. Boone would hope.

Jacob smiles back with a glint in his eye. "Deal. I've got my car.

Do you need a ride?"

Genevieve shrugs. "I was going to take the bus."

Jacob smiles. "Come with me." He starts to pack up his bag.

"I mean, we can wait till class is over. We've only got eleven more minutes," Genevieve whispers.

"Genevieve, world domination waits for no one. It can't be dragged down by multivariate whatsit hoo-ha." Jacob winks.

Genevieve laughs harder than the joke was funny. Dr. Boone doesn't seem to notice the distraction, but his TA glares at them from her seat near the chalkboard.

Genevieve quietly packs her bag too and tiptoes behind Jacob out of the lecture hall with a full nine minutes left of their three-hour class. Missing class isn't her MO, but she wasn't going to pass up a chance to finally hang out with Jacob.

Their scurry down the corridor is interrupted by a shrill, "Hey! Jacob!"

Genevieve and Jacob turn around. It's the sour-faced TA. Seriously. Apparently she's a hall monitor, too, which Genevieve didn't even think was a thing in college.

She slithers toward them. "Hey, Jacob, I've been meaning to talk to you. We really need to catch up!"

What? This has to be above a TA's paygrade.

Genevieve looks her up and down. Grey hoodie, blue headband in her carefully parted blonde hair. Delicate eyeglasses. Heart-shaped mouth. Both arms suddenly wrapped around one of Jacob's. Genevieve's heart thumps.

"It's been forever," the girl coos at Jacob.

"Another time. I have somewhere to be," Jacob looks toward the door, their escape to the outside world.

Genevieve tucks her short hair behind her ear, mouth agape.

Jacob's arm leech doesn't so much as glance at Genevieve. "Yeah, I know it's awkward having me for your TA. And that class is so boring." The girl rolls her eyes at Jacob.

"Yeah, well, I've gotta go, Laur."

The girl grimaces for a moment, then smiles from ear to ear. "Well, you need to call me soon!"

"Uhh, sure."

Laura lets go of Jacob then opens her arms for a hug. Genevieve just stands there, invisible. That familiar lion rises inside as she endures their too-long hug.

Jacob breaks away first and heads down the last twenty feet of hallway, motioning Genevieve to come with him. "See ya!" he yells without looking back.

They cross the crunchy lawn in silence and then head down a flight of concrete stairs to the student parking lot.

"Hey, sorry about that. I don't know what Laura's deal is. She's weird. She's the one who broke up with me."

Genevieve looks down at the icy stairs. Just to keep from slipping, she tells herself.

"Well, she looks like she doesn't know when it's time to move on."

Jacob stops in the street. "We broke up over six months ago. She recommended the class because she was TA-ing it, but I didn't know she would be weird."

"So am I supposed to expect a parade of girls to be constantly throwing themselves at you? Because that's *not* my idea of a good time."

Jacob just folds his arms and smiles. "Noted. You let a guy know where he stands, Genevieve."

Genevieve's shoulders relax.

After walking a few yards in the parking lot, they stop at what might be the most pathetic car Genevieve has ever seen, some beige 1980's-era Honda Civic hatchback. And what is that on the passenger door handle? Is that—? Is that duct tape?

Jacob pulls on the jimmy-rigged handle of Genevieve's door with a creak. One side of the handle pulls loose, and Jacob has to kneel down to tape it back into place before opening the door for Genevieve. Genevieve suppresses a giggle. The lion recedes.

"Hey! Don't laugh! I'm a college student with a steady diet of ramen and potatoes and big plans! I won't be driving The Kraken forever. She's served me well. She's gone over 270,000 miles, but she never breaks down."

Genevieve snickers as she climbs inside. "Except for her door handle."

Jacob gets in through the driver's side and turns the key in the ignition to the sound of The Kraken stalling. He tries again. It wheezes and stalls. The third time's a charm and a relief. Genevieve howls with laughter.

Jacob furls his brow. "Okay, yeah. You know what? I have zero debt. I don't want to impress people with a flashy car that's bleeding me dry. I want to live like a pauper so I can be a king someday. Without the stress of debt. That's my goal."

Genevieve looks over at Jacob. His wide eyes seem to be asking her something. "I actually think that's really cool, Jacob. Really. I don't know a lot of people with that kind of... determination."

Jacob beams. He pulls the car down the street. Interspersed with directions to Genevieve's house, which she keeps forgetting to give until Jacob has missed a turn, they talk nonstop about music, hobbies, goals, dreams, people. At Genevieve's house they overcook the spaghetti then spend hours scheming as they attempt to eat their semi-palatable concoction on the couch in the front room. When Genevieve's mom hobbles in, complaining of her backache and oversharing her frustrations about *what your father did with the money this time*, Jacob appears unfazed. He doesn't seem to mind the shabby house or pretend to gag or make fun of Genevieve when she confides her love of musicals to him. He even asks her to download a couple of her favorite songs from *Wicked* on her laptop, and then at least pretends to like them as he listens with her.

When Genevieve yawns, feeling safe in her own home for once, she glances at her watch. 2:18 AM. Dang it! She's got to be at her early shift at the grocery store in four hours.

"I hate to say this, but I really have to go to bed."

"Oh, yeah, of course. It's late. This has been— This has been amazing. I haven't had this much fun in a really long time."

Genevieve's fingers tingle. "We should do it again."

"I would *love* that."

Jacob stands up but doesn't walk toward the door. He seems to consider something before he asks, "Hey, can I just show you something? It's like— I've never shown it to anyone before."

"Never? What about Laura?" Genevieve teases, but her

stomach tightens.

"No, not even Laura. She knew about it, but she never saw it." Jacob looks at her with those wide questioning eyes again. Something important seems to be happening.

"Sure. Show me."

Jacob walks right out the front door without saying goodbye.

Well, that was different. Before she decides whether or not to follow him, Jacob rushes back through the door without knocking, holding a flash drive in the air.

"I had to get this from my car. I wrote a novel," he confesses.

Genevieve sits up, wide awake. *"You wrote a novel?"*

"Uh-huh."

"Like, past tense? A book? You wrote a whole book?"

"Yeah. It's 362 pages in Word. It's still not perfect, but I've written like five drafts so far."

"You wrote FIVE DRAFTS of a 362-page novel?"

"Is that weird?"

"No! That's cool! How did you find time? You know, with school and work and everything?"

Jacob beams, his cheeks pink. "I just had to write it. I figure if you're really passionate about doing something, you make the time. Do you want to see it?"

"Uh, yeah. Definitely. Jacob, you are full of surprises."

Jacob inserts the flash drive into the laptop they downloaded music on hours earlier and tilts the screen toward Genevieve. She reads and reads, wrapped up in the story and in the guy who wrote it. She reads until after her last bus has come and gone.

Jacob drops her straight at the store, ten minutes late for her 6:00 AM shift.

1   Resch, Marley N., and Kevin G. Alderson. "Female Partners of Men Who Use Pornography: Are Honesty and Mutual Use Associated With Relationship Satisfaction?." *Journal of Sex & Marital Therapy* 40, no. 5 (2014): 410-424.

7. THE TALK

Knowing is half the battle.
  —G.I. Joe

WENDY

I met Penny on a park bench on a sunny September morning. An enthusiastic thirty-six-year-old in a ponytail and chunky plastic glasses, she'd been emailing with me for about a week. She wanted to tell me about the time she had The Talk with a guy.

But let's back up. About six months earlier, Penny attended one of Adam's lectures on navigating the effects of a partner's porn use. At the time she'd had little experience with porn; she only sat in on the class to support a friend. But she held onto her notes because she couldn't shake the feeling she'd need them. "Maybe someone I know will date a porn addict someday. Maybe this will help them," she thought.

Months later, Penny met a guy on Tinder. She'd met guys online before, but she'd never been so giddy about a date. He seemed sweet and talented and attractive. She was so excited that she figured it couldn't possibly work out. But then after a shy, awkward first date, they agreed to see each other again. By their second date, they were laughing and talking all night. Soon, he started sending Penny recordings of songs he'd sung and played on the guitar each night.

On the third date they held hands for the first time. Also on that date, Edwin, full of trepidation, told Penny about his compulsive pornography use.

We met Edwin two chapters ago, when he told me how his fiancée ghosted him after he confessed his porn habit to her. He was determined to never break a girl's heart (or his own) that way again. So when he found himself quickly falling for Penny, he had to tell her. He was terrified, but he somehow managed to get the words out. This time it was different.

Penny just hugged him tight and said, "Thank you for telling me."

Penny wasn't a fan of pornography. But after hearing Adam's lecture and doing some reading, she considered the possibility that she might someday date a person who'd struggled with porn use.

Penny's also pretty analytical. She's a planner. She'd kept and organized the notes from Adam's presentation. Thus far, not much had changed for Edwin. He'd sought almost no outside help with his compulsion, other than attending his church's addiction recovery class off and on. But the porn use persisted.

So after Penny squeezed him tight and let him know she appreciated his honesty, she remembered those notes from Adam's presentation. That night at 11 PM, Penny and Edwin drove to her house and found the notes. Together, they read over the four steps of The Talk.

STEP ONE: IT'S OKAY IF IT ISN'T PERFECT

ADAM

Your story might be like Penny's. Maybe in the interest of courage and transparency, your partner already filled you in that he's been having trouble staying away from porn. If he did, kudos to him, because it's no small feat to share vulnerable details that might upend your relationship.

Or maybe you haven't yet discussed pornography—possibly because it hasn't played much of a role in your partner's life, or perhaps because he doesn't know how to tell you about his struggles. Either way, The Talk is a vital step to help you better understand the extent of the problem and make decisions about where to go from there.

And remember, as with your warm-up talk, perfection isn't the goal here.

In second grade, I was somehow coerced into playing the piano at a school talent show. My mom had made me take lessons for about two years up to that point, so I guess I was decent enough to play in public. I was terrified of what the kids in the audience would think of me. I don't know about your peers growing up, but mine mocked each other relentlessly over the tiniest things. Kids are mean. I could probably have used some therapy. But I digress.

I practiced. A lot. I probably practiced that short little piece dozens of times before the show. After nervously sitting down in front of six hundred kids, I performed my song. And despite those hours of practice, I made a huge mistake, right in the middle. It was big enough that I lost track of what I was doing. Embarrassed, I hid my face in my hands for a moment. I couldn't decide whether to pretend that the mistake was intentional or if I should just plan on putting a "for sale" sign in front of my house. I decided to clumsily finish the piece.

Amazingly, I took another ten years of piano lessons after that, and I even performed in public many more times. My friends turned out to be more forgiving than I had expected. Nobody mocked me, and some of them even came up afterward to tell me I did a good job.

No matter how much you practice and prepare for this conversation, it won't be perfect. Penny would tell you that her conversation with Edwin (or any of their subsequent discussions) wasn't tidy or by the book, either. However, The Talk brought them closer together and was a game-changer for their relationship.

So the first step of The Talk is to just breathe. It will be okay.

STEP TWO: SHARE

Before you ask any questions, begin by sharing your own feelings and experience. Sharing opens the door to emotional intimacy; this conversation can be very bonding if you both let it. If you forget everything else in the moment, remember the paradox from Chapter Four: be compassionate and understanding, as well as committed to standing up for your own needs.

The four points you should share:

- Express how you feel about pornography
- Explain what you need in this relationship
- Expose your own experience
- Emphasize your commitment to your partner

EXPRESS YOUR FEELINGS

To start off, share your elevator pitch about porn once more. Maybe go into a bit more detail here if you're feeling it—why it's important to you to discuss your concerns about pornography, how you feel that it objectifies people, how it steals attention from relationships, how it's a way for people to self-medicate when they should be seeking healthier avenues to deal with their pain—everything you learned about pornography in Chapters One and Three. Just keep it simple.

EXPLAIN YOUR NEEDS

Most women who've had these conversations tell me that they have two basic needs: honesty (yep—here's honesty again) and emotional safety.

So remind him how much more important honesty is to your relationship than anything he's seen or done. You can also remind him that hiding things from you isn't protecting you.

Emotional safety is the freedom to feel your feelings and express them without fear of blowing the relationship up. Ask him to try to understand your feelings. And promise him that you'll do the same for him.

He might be experiencing emotions himself, like shame, fear, sadness, frustration, or something else entirely during The Talk. He's human. Those emotions are valid. Just ask him to avoid becoming defensive, and don't become defensive yourself. If either of you become aggravated, it might kill The Talk for now. But if you're kind, patient, and understanding with each other, you'll feel safe together.

EXPOSE YOUR OWN EXPERIENCE

This is the perfect opportunity for you to share your own experiences with sexual imagery and behaviors. If you ask him to share the most private details of his life without revealing any of yours, The Talk will become an interrogation. Nobody wants to be interrogated. It sets up a parent-child power dynamic when you want to be equals. So be honest yourself.

If you have a history of exposure to pornography or even your own compulsive porn use, this is when you would bring that up. There still seems to be an enormous stigma about women compulsively using pornography and other erotic media. Women are often portrayed as the gatekeepers of virtue, the ones who aren't supposed to act on sexual impulses, even though it's not uncommon for women to have their own battles with pornography's allure.

Or, if compulsive sexual fantasy has ever been a distraction for you, consider sharing that. Many women are more likely to fantasize, either in romance novels or their own heads, than in overt pornography viewing.*[1] If you have a history of sexual fantasy invading your thoughts, making it difficult to be present and focus on the important aspects of life, share that with him. Whether it's been in your mind or on a screen, this is where you talk about it.

Remember, this isn't some sort of twisted confession or evaluation of whether your sexual history is "normal" or not. This is about discussing the types of sexual thoughts, images, or behaviors that could get in the way of a real sexual relationship.

---

* This isn't just folklore; there is real research to back this notion up. In 2015, researchers found that women experience elevated levels of testosterone (yep, women have testosterone too) when they are having sex, anticipating having sex, or even when they're simply fantasizing about sex. But women don't experience elevated testosterone when they're viewing pornography (even though men do).

Secrets keep people stuck.

If your own sexual experiences aren't extensive enough for you to know what struggles you might have someday, just be honest about that and mention that you're willing to pay attention and learn how you may need to grow down the road.

All of this will take a good amount of bravery on your part, but the more open and honest you can be about your own past, the safer he will feel sharing his experience with you.

EMPHASIZE YOUR COMMITMENT

Finally, share your commitment to him. You can't promise that you're going to stay in the relationship no matter what, because there are no guarantees when you're just dating. You don't know what he'll share or how you'll respond to it.

But you *can* promise to carefully consider his feelings, to examine your own emotions, to treat your relationship with care and importance. You can promise that you're committed to the conversation and that you won't just run at the first sign he's had experience with porn.

STEP THREE: THE SEVEN QUESTIONS

The Talk may be one of the more intensive conversations you've had with each other. As you can imagine, this discussion could go on for hours or lose focus if you don't have some way to rein it in. We're giving you seven key questions to ask to help structure The Talk so it stays as productive as possible.

These questions should determine the role pornography has played and may still be playing in your future husband's life. Again, this shouldn't be an interrogation—it's not about unearthing every detail about everything he's ever done or seen, including who he had a crush on in fourth grade. And if you forget some questions in the moment, or a question or two leads to further discussion, that's all right. This conversation won't be your last one about pornography.

Below are the seven questions to cover. It might feel more natural if you answer these questions as well, so he doesn't feel like he's under the spotlight.

1. When were you first exposed to pornography?
2. How often have you viewed it since then?
3. How often do you view it now?
4. What feelings make you most vulnerable to turning back to pornography? (These feelings could be sadness, loneliness, anger, anxiety, shame, or others.)
5. How have you given yourself permission to turn back to porn? (Examples might be: "I'm not hurting anyone." "Porn isn't real; at least I'm not doing anything with real people." "This is the last time I'll look." "It's not really affecting my life that much." "I can stop anytime I want.")
6. What ways have you tried to eliminate porn from your life? What has and hasn't worked?
7. How do you feel pornography affects your life and well-being?

Take these questions slowly. Give him ample time to think about and respond to each question. If you're both answering the questions, you might want to answer first to help him feel comfortable. It's okay to sit in silence for a while. Any of these questions could bring up difficult memories and emotions. Feel free to say something to the effect of, "Please take your time. I know this isn't what you usually discuss with people. I'd rather slow down and make sure we understand each other than try to rush this." And feel free to share more about your own experience when it's relevant.

STEP FOUR: RESPOND

Don't try to solve any problems in the course of this conversation. We're used to expecting easy resolutions. In a ninety-minute romantic comedy, two lovable protagonists despise each other at first, then fall madly in love, then have to work through the devastating realization that one of them has been telling a big lie the entire time, which they overcome with public declarations of love at a crowded airport minutes before our heroine is about to board a plane for France. And then they live happily ever after.

Real life doesn't resolve itself so tidily after a ninety-minute rollercoaster of romantic tension. You'll both need time to think about what the answers to these questions mean and what to do about it. That's what the rest of the book is for. For now, simply finish The Talk with some variation of these three statements.

1. "THANK YOU."

No matter how The Talk goes, you need to thank this good man for taking you seriously enough to talk to you about something that matters to you. He invested time and energy into this, and that counts for a lot. Help him see that you value his contribution to the relationship, which will increase the chances he'll want to talk again in the future.

2. "I MAY NEED SOME TIME."

Since you have no idea what emotions you'll have about what he shares, just be prepared to tell him that you need some extra time to process how you feel. It can be as simple as, "I may need some time to work through what I'm feeling, but please know that I am so grateful to you for sharing. This means more to me than you can imagine."

3. "IF THERE'S ANYTHING ELSE, PLEASE SHARE."

This invites a crucial ongoing dialogue. Rather than wondering whether you should have worked some mind voodoo to coerce every last detail out of him, just offer an open invitation to share more in the future. Let him know that you understand he must have been nervous answering all those questions, and that when people are nervous, they can neglect to share all of the important information the relationship needs to grow. Down the road, if he remembers something he forgot to tell you, you're asking him to please share at that point.

This way, if he shares *almost* everything with you and later decides he's ready to tell you more, the door is always open. It will make future conversations easier. Please know that it's normal, especially in developing relationships, for people to disclose information over time, rather than in a single episode. So, very simply, you could say, "Hey, I know this has been pretty intense today. I realize later you might remember something else you forgot to say. Please, as soon as you remember, just come talk to me. It will help me feel like you understand how important this is to me."

If your future husband shares more with you later than he initially did, it doesn't mean anything catastrophic. It doesn't mean your relationship is over or that he's a compulsive liar. It means he's learning to take risks opening up about events he may have hidden all of his life.

However The Talk ends, we hope you'll feel proud of yourselves for being so brave. You've opened lines to vital communication in your relationship. What you may not be prepared for is the surprising range of emotions that will likely come in the following hours and even days after the conversation. In the next chapter, we'll address unexpected emotions that may arise and what to do about them.

GENEVIEVE   SEPTEMBER 2006

Genevieve chases her dad down the stairs and across the kitchen, catching up to him in the front doorway. She grabs the curling iron sticking out from the pile of clothes and shoes he can barely carry. He stops to let her pull the long cord from his grasp. "What do you need that for? You don't even have long hair."

"Dad, it's Mara's only curling iron. She uses it every single day."

"Well, fine. Take it. Are you gonna help me get set up?"

Genevieve suppresses an eyeroll. "No. Dad. This is your— I'm not a part of this. I gotta go." She runs back upstairs, shouting over her shoulder, "Ask me before you try to sell my stuff next time, okay?"

"Jenny, c'mon, just give me a hand."

"Jacob's coming over in a minute. And don't call me Jenny," she yells as she turns the corner and he disappears out of sight.

Not *in* a minute. *For* a minute. When Jacob called half an hour ago to see if Genevieve was home, he said he was coming over *for* a minute. Which is strange, come to think of it, since he doesn't have class on Saturdays, and they'd talked about spending the day together.

Genevieve opens her closet to find it half empty. *This is not happening.*

"Dad!" Genevieve shouts as she leaps back down the stairs, across the kitchen, and out the front door in about five steps total.

"Dad! Hey! Did you go in *my* closet?"

And there it all is, laid out neatly on a folding table on the front lawn: Genevieve's favorite dress that Grandma gave her for Christmas, her last stain-free white button-down shirt, her porcelain Eiffel Tower figurine, three pairs of her shoes...

"MY SHOES, DAD?!" Genevieve purses her lips, barely swallowing the biting words that want to fly from her mouth. She bundles everything of hers she can find into her arms.

"Now, Jenny. I didn't want to tell you kids yet. I don't want to upset Mara if she has to change schools—"

"'But your mother and I have decided we might be moving.'" Genevieve sing-songs, rolling her eyes. "Save your stories for Mom. I know you're losing the house. I know you're trying to keep it from all of us, Mom included. Who do you think takes those notices off our front door before Mom finds them?" Genevieve spins around, her cheeks hot, shouting, "And don't call me Jen—" and runs smack into Jacob, almost dropping her pile of recovered treasures. "Oh, hey!"

"Hey."

Genevieve leads the way back toward the front door. "I, uhh... What's up? I'm so glad you're here. My dad is driving me completely crazy. He's taking everything without asking. I don't know if he thinks a yard sale will make enough money to bring the mortgage up to date, or if it'll be easier to move if we have less stuff, or what. I heard him making promises he can't keep to Mom last night. I had to rescue Mara's curling iron..." Genevieve looks up at Jacob's stony face.

"I'm really sorry." He looks off to the side, hands in his pockets, brow furrowed.

"Jacob?" Genevieve's heart thumps.

Jacob glances over at the pile in Genevieve's arms. "Oh. Let me carry that for you."

Jacob reaches for the pile, but Genevieve pulls back. "Oh, I've got it. I was just gonna... Jacob? Are you okay?"

"Me? Ummm...." He pulls a folded-up piece of paper from his pocket. "Here." He looks down at his toes. His mouth twists as he mumbles, "Just read it when I'm gone. I gotta go."

He hands it to Genevieve and doesn't seem to notice that she can barely grab it with her not-quite spare hand that's also holding the heel of a shoe.

He turns around and walks back to his beat-up Civic without so much as a goodbye.

Genevieve just stands there, watching him drive down the street.

Then she drops the entire pile on the ground as his car turns the corner and disappears out of sight.

When Genevieve's wits return, she grabs the paper from the ground and runs into the house, tears streaming onto her chin, leaving her belongings strewn on the front walk as the first yard sale patrons pull up to her house.

Genevieve slams and locks her bedroom door behind her. She's had breakups before. But not like this. Not with Jacob.

Plus, what kind of baby has the audacity to end it in a letter? Just last week he'd left little notes for her to find all over the place. One under her car visor that read, "Guess what? You're my favorite person in the world." "My life is better with you in it," in her sweatshirt pocket. "Genevieve + Jacob 4 Ever" under her pillow. She was just starting to imagine a long, wonderful life with him. Genevieve's head spins. What the heck happened?

She sits down on her bed with her back against the corner of the wall, trying to breathe past the stabbing lump in her chest. She closes her eyes for a second so that her pounding head doesn't explode, then unfolds the typed letter on her legs.

Genevieve,

This is by far the scariest thing I've ever done. I realize that this might be the end of everything we've built together. I care about you—more than you know. That's why I need to tell you something that I've hardly ever shared with anyone. I completely understand if you decide that you don't want to stay with me.

I have a problem with pornography. It's more than a little problem. I'm pretty sure it's an addiction. I want to stop, so bad. But I can't. I've tried to stop, tons of times. Sometimes I can go weeks without looking, but somehow I always get sucked back in. I don't know what's wrong with me. I waste hours watching porn during the day when I should be doing something productive. Sometimes I stay up all night watching porn and hardly sleep at all. I truly am trying to stop. I don't want it in my life. But I can't seem to break this habit, and I don't want it to end up hurting you.

Ever since I met you, I've been thinking about this day. I've hoped that somehow I would fix my problem before I ever had to tell you about it. But I'm still struggling, and it's not fair to you to keep this from you.

I love you. I see you as someone I'd love to marry someday. I think you're amazing. But I don't want to hold you back. I understand if you don't want this in your life. You already have plenty of stress. Maybe piling this on top isn't worth it to you.

Genevieve, I desperately want to stop

succumbing to porn. I want us to be together. But I don't want you to have to deal with this beast like I have for so many years. I don't blame you at all if you decide this isn't worth the pain. I promise to try as hard as I can to put this behind me. I also know it's not going to be easy, and I understand if you need to move on. Please take as much time as you need. I'll leave you alone until you're ready to talk and let me know what you've decided.

Yours always,
Jacob

Genevieve is still. She squeezes her eyes closed as the tears keep pouring. But the dread has seeped out of the room. Warmth has taken its place.

Genevieve takes a deep breath, wipes the tears from her cheeks with the back of her wrists, and for the third time today, races down the stairs and out the front door, grabbing the keys to the Hummer off the kitchen table. She leaps over her scattered belongings blowing in the wind and past the scavengers pawing through her family's possessions. She jumps in the car, ignoring her dad's shouts of, "Hey, Jenny, can you help this guy over here—"

1   Goldey, Katherine L., and Sari M. van Anders. "Identification with Stimuli Moderates Women's Affective and Testosterone Responses to Self-Chosen Erotica." *Archives of Sexual Behavior* (2015): 1-17.

8. PERMISSION TO FEEL

Our feelings are our most genuine paths to knowledge.
  —Audre Lorde

ADAM

We need to talk about your feelings now.

Don't worry, I'm not going to make you lie on a couch in my office and drudge up childhood memories of your father. The fact is, when you have The Talk, you may hear things you weren't expecting. And you may *feel* things you weren't expecting.

Emotions are important messengers. Without getting too technical here, let's just say that the emotional part of your brain is quite an efficient communicator—much more so than your rational brain. There will be plenty of times throughout your life when you'll feel emotions long before you have any idea why you feel that way.

For example, let's imagine you're out for a Sunday drive, and you see the flashing lights of a cop car in your rearview mirror. If you're like me, your palms start to sweat, your heart pounds, and you instinctively put your foot on the brake. Only after this sequence of events do you check to see if you were speeding. Maybe you weren't. But at the sight of those red and blue flashes, your emotions communicated that you were in trouble before your thinking brain caught up.

So our fears help us get to safety. We also feel anger to help defend ourselves, sadness to process loss, disgust to avoid substances that might harm us. And because our emotions fire so quickly, they often surprise us.

No matter what you feel, it's important to acknowledge that your emotions are real and there's a reason you feel the way you do. Your feelings don't have to dictate your actions or decisions, but when you encounter an uncomfortable emotion, the first step is to listen to those feelings rather than suppress them, because they're trying to tell you something.

If you discover that your partner can't kick a pornography habit, a potential threat to your relationship, you'll likely have emotions about it. You may even have quite a few emotions.

And your feelings might change from hour to hour or even from minute to minute. One moment, you might feel content or optimistic. And then out of nowhere, you feel terrified, depressed, sad, disappointed, angry. And there might come a point when you start to wonder, "Why are my emotions changing all the time? Am I crazy?" Don't worry. This is all normal.

Your emotions are messengers signaling, among other things, your unmet needs. When you're lonely, the unmet need might be companionship. When you feel angry, your need might be better boundaries to protect yourself from being hurt. When you're afraid, your need might be more predictability, safety, or a sense of control.

But what if you don't feel anything? What if you're unfazed by learning that your significant other has a compulsive porn habit? That's okay too. Whether they're positive, negative, or seemingly non-existent, when it comes to emotions, the unexpected is normal.

CASE EXAMPLES: TONYA AND PENNY

WENDY

Let me show you what this looks like:

A chatty and enthusiastic woman named Tonya sat with me on her couch while her toddler daughter and my preschooler climbed all over the two of us. Tonya struck me as younger than her thirty years of life, despite her troubled past. Her soft-spoken husband, John, sat across the room on an ottoman. Together, she and John detailed his struggle with pornography.

John was working toward recovery from porn use, but he still relapsed from time to time. Before John, Tonya was married to Freddie, another porn user. But Freddie also had demons much nastier than porn—he cheated on and abused Tonya. Freddie blindsided Tonya when he told her he had a girlfriend the night before Tonya gave birth to their second son. Devastated and alone, with two young sons to care for, Tonya ended their marriage shortly thereafter.

When Tonya married John five years later, she knew about his compulsions. But she loved him and hoped she wasn't making the same mistake again. She didn't want to endure that horror a second time. For a while, John appeared to be in recovery. But a year into their marriage, when they were meeting with their pastor, John broke down and asked if he could speak with the pastor in private. He confessed that he was still viewing pornography. The pastor urged him to tell his wife. Before Tonya left the church that night, the pastor gave her a heads-up that John would be sharing some hard news, and he asked her to be kind and understanding. That night, when John confessed to Tonya that he'd been keeping his current porn use from her, Tonya did feel compassion for John. She recalled feeling peaceful and close to John.

But the next morning, Tonya felt irate, even though nothing had changed. Outrage and despair drowned out all of the peace, optimism, and goodwill she felt toward John the night before, which makes sense. Even though John isn't Freddie, Tonya's feelings were communicating to her that she might be in the same danger she was in with Freddie, the addict, cheater, and abuser.

Even though Tonya wanted to be understanding, she couldn't ignore what her body was telling her.

Contrast that with Penny, who we met in the last chapter, the one who was dating Edwin after his fiancée ghosted him. When Penny found out about Edwin's compulsions, she had very little experience with pornography. She started attending a twelve-step group for partners of compulsive porn users, where at times she felt out of place. Many of the women were deep in their trauma. And Penny didn't feel particularly traumatized. She felt fine. That response was understandable, considering how little porn use had affected her life up to that point.

SUPPRESSED EMOTIONS AND MANGLED HOT DOGS

ADAM

The bottom line here is that whatever you're feeling, even if it makes no sense at all, is completely normal. Feeling angry is normal. Feeling sad is normal. Feeling afraid is normal. Feeling forgiving and compassionate is normal. Feeling hopeful is normal. Feeling confused and conflicted is normal. Feeling nothing at all is normal. And in fact, even feeling many of those emotions at the same time is normal.

So let's just agree on something right now: we're not going to judge your emotions. I want you to be kind to yourself above all else. Because the moment you start trying to convince the feeling part of your brain that it doesn't have a right to feel, your internal defenses go up. And part of your brain retorts, "I should be able to feel whatever I want!" No one likes to be told how to feel, even when we're the ones doing it to ourselves. So give yourself permission to feel whatever you're feeling.

Have you ever tried to cook a hot dog in the microwave? If you cook it long enough, it will basically explode. Even the times when it doesn't fly to smithereens, you'll hear a loud pop, and it will rip wide open, tear straight down the middle. A hot dog has a sealed outer membrane that holds together that meat-like substance on the inside, so when you apply heat to it, the fluids inside the dog turn to steam, and the pressure has nowhere to go. Eventually, it goes off like a bomb, and you end up with a mangled concoction that resembles a swollen, broken finger. The solution is to poke some holes in it or slice it down the middle to release that pressure while it cooks.

Now please note here that I am not condoning eating hot dogs, since no one really knows what they're made of. But my point is, if there's nowhere for the pressure to go, then—BOOM. Likewise, if you try to ignore your emotions, pressure will build.

WENDY

Suppressing your emotions comes with some scary health risks and takes a toll on your relationships. People who repress anger are twice as likely to suffer from heart disease. And researchers have found that couples who suppress their anger toward each other have shorter lifespans than those who express it.[1]

But here's a catch-22: giving in to all of your feelings has some consequences of its own. If you suddenly feel angry one day about your boyfriend's pornography use, and you go out and key his car or have a red-faced screaming match with him, it could negatively affect your health (as well as his car). You have *three times* the risk of a stroke or blood clot in the two hours following an angry outburst.[2]

HOW TO MANAGE AND EXPRESS EMOTIONS

So here's the plan: you're going to share your emotions in a healthy, constructive way.

Sharing emotions with people you care about is one of the healthiest ways to manage your feelings. In fact, positive communication, which includes openly sharing feelings, is the *single most common* trait happy couples share.[3] So don't bottle those emotions. Share them. We'll give you three strategies to share your emotions in a healthy way.

1. GIVE YOURSELF TIME

Breathe. Because your emotions are messengers communicating

something important, if you can figure out what that message is and fill your partner in, you'll be ahead of the game. However, if you feel intense anger, fear, or other challenging emotions, you may need to take some time to sit with those emotions and examine them before you share them with your partner. That way, your conversation about them is more likely to be constructive and clear.

So breathe. Breathing is one of the best ways to calm your anxiety. Inhaling activates your sympathetic nervous system, which arouses you, primes you for action, etc., while exhaling activates your parasympathetic nervous system, which relaxes and soothes you. Trauma researchers have found that people with PTSD struggle to regulate their sympathetic and parasympathetic nervous systems, and that learning to just breathe helps to heal their trauma symptoms.[4] If you can find time to sit with your emotions and breathe in and out slowly, it will help you to reflect on your emotional state.

If you find your emotions are quite intense, feel free to sleep on them before sharing them with your partner. I don't know who came up with the advice, "Never go to bed angry," but sometimes the best thing you can do when you're angry is get a good night's sleep if you're able. Time and a night's rest may help you approach your emotions more calmly.

If you take time, sleep on your emotions, and still feel intensely emotional, to the point that you can't calm yourself down, you may need to seek professional help. A counselor can help you work through whatever is causing your distress before you address it with your partner.

2. WRITE

Take time to write about your emotions. Don't just rage-write— this can actually make you more upset. Write analytically about your emotions. Try to see yourself from an outsider's perspective. Examine what you're feeling. Ask yourself why you might feel the way you do. Consider any circumstances or events in your life, past or present, that might be creating your emotional state.

Writing about your emotions can be another powerful tool

to process your unpredictable feelings. Studies have found that people who take time to write about their deepest emotions and the most traumatic events of their lives experience long-term increases in physical and mental well-being in a range of categories, from reduced blood pressure and symptoms of depression to improved GPA, memory, mood, and fewer sick days at work.[5]

And whether or not you're experiencing heightened emotions, take time to fill out Appendix A at the back of the book. It will help you examine your emotions about pornography and your relationship generally, and you may discover new aspects of your emotional world.

3. SHARE THE EMOTION

Address the emotion with your partner once you've had the time to breathe, write, and reflect. It helps to perform something psychologist John Gottman likes to call a "soft start-up."

Gottman is among the most notable psychologists alive as well as *the* communication guru. He studied conflict for six years with fellow psychologist Sybil Carrère and discovered that he could predict whether a couple would get divorced based on the first three minutes of a disagreement (hint: if one or both members of the couple exhibits contempt toward the other, the marriage may be in dire trouble, even if they otherwise look like a great couple), and that ninety-four percent of interactions end the same way they begin (i.e., if they start out happy, angry, blaming, etc., they'll end that way too).

Sharing your emotions with your partner won't necessarily lead to conflict. But because the discussion could involve tension and painful feelings, start softly. According to Gottman, a soft start-up should avoid casting blame. Use "I" statements to talk about how you're feeling, rather than "you" statements to blame your partner for perceived wrongs. However you need to say it, think of the best way to minimize the chance your partner will get defensive. And avoid what Gottman calls The Four Horsemen, which can be fatal to positive communication: criticism, contempt, defensiveness, and stonewalling.[6]

LET HIM KNOW HE DOESN'T NEED TO FIX YOUR PAIN

ADAM

Here's a tip: anticipate that your future husband may try to "fix" your painful emotions. Research has shown that men have more difficulty tolerating uncomfortable emotions and discussing relationship problems than women do,[*][7] so often a man's knee-jerk response will be to fix your problem and make it instantly better.

So share the secret sauce with him: let him know that you need him to say, "I'm so sorry. I'm here for you." And that's it. Of course, he should be sincere and use his own words. But tell him that what you really need is for him to empathize with your pain and commit to stick with you as you struggle. And if you need anything more than that, you'll let him know.

I want you to understand that your future husband also has permission to feel whatever emotions he's experiencing. He might feel a good bit of fear of his own about his secrets being exposed, about the future of your relationship, etc. He may express his fears in a variety of ways. He might even seem a bit aloof or distant from you. So if you notice that he's having a hard time, cut him some slack as well. Be patient and give *him* permission to process and express his emotions with you. And don't be surprised if it feels a bit like pulling teeth to get him to share his emotions. As we'll discuss in Chapter Eleven, many men haven't been socialized to share their emotions in the way women have. It may take some work. But for both of you, learning to pay attention to and feel your respective feelings will start you on the path to self-awareness.

JACOB   SEPTEMBER 2006

Jacob sets his keys on his dresser, falls into bed, and just lies there, a six-foot-two lump of dead weight, even as the late-morning

---

[*] In seventy-one heterosexual couples, researchers tested skin conductance while men and women discussed relationship problems with each other. The men experienced significantly greater physiological arousal when discussing relationship problems than the women did.

sunlight streams through his eyelids. That's that, then. He never even told Laura, not after they dated almost a year.

But he couldn't keep it from Genevieve. He was hoping to marry her. He rubs his eyes, letting his hands rest on them. Maybe he's meant to be alone. Maybe that's the price he has to pay.

Man, Genevieve was the easiest person to talk to. She understood him like nobody else had. And she was so certain of herself, of what she wanted. She made him feel *important*.

But for weeks, as he'd daydreamed of a life with Genevieve, he hadn't slept at night. His thoughts would run in circles, trying to find a way around it. Maybe if he could quit porn for long enough, he could tell her all about it someday, after it was an old story from a different life. But in the end, he couldn't ignore the voice that screamed his magical cure wasn't coming. Genevieve had told him every gruesome detail about her life, and Jacob owed her the same. So he typed the letter yesterday and sealed his fate. She wouldn't sign up for a life like this.

The doorbell rings, but Jacob can't will himself to get up. Greg will get it. It's always for Greg, anyway.

She's probably read the letter by now. How hurt will she be? For all his writing, he didn't know how to comfort her with his words. Not about this.

Without so much as a knock, Greg pokes his head through Jacob's door across the room. "Door's for you. Whoa, you okay, man?"

Jacob lifts his heavy head. "Fine. Who is it?"

"That one girl."

Jacob sits up straight. "What one girl? Genevieve? The girl I've been dating for five months?"

"Uhh, yeah. I think so."

Jacob's feet are on the floor and out of the room, almost before he is. Why didn't she read the letter yet?

Jacob scans the empty front room. "Where is she?"

"Uhh, she's waiting for you outside."

"Why didn't you let her in?!"

Jacob yanks open the front door. It's Genevieve, all right, with blotchy cheeks and wet eyes. Add a black dress, and you'd think she was on her way to a funeral.

His funeral. His heart races. "Genevieve? Did you—?"

She barely nods. Then she throws her arms around Jacob's neck and presses her cheek against his shoulder. He stands still, paralyzed. Why isn't she angry? She should be upset.

Her heart beats against his ribs. "Are you so dumb to believe that I would just give up and leave you like that?"

His face feels warm.

She whispers, "You could have told me all of that to my face ages ago."

He still can't move.

"Jacob?" Genevieve searches his face.

She's... going to stay. It finally sinks in. He exhales and pulls her close. "I'm— I'm sorry. *I'm so sorry.*"

"Don't be sorry. Next time you have something big to tell me, just tell me. You don't have to hold onto it." She pulls back and looks him in the eye with her signature fierce glint. "We're going to overcome this. Together."

Jacob's head spins. He feels like he could float away. This is it. Everything he'd ever worried about... It's all over now. He thought he'd be stuck his whole life, forever damaged. But with this thing he and Genevieve have, maybe they can conquer anything together.

He pulls her close again. "Genevieve, I never thought— I'm just really— You and me—"

"Just stop talking."

So he holds her in the open doorway, hardly believing what can happen in the space of twenty minutes.

1   Harburg, Ernest, Niko Kaciroti, Lillian Gleiberman, Mara Julius, and M. Anthony Schork. "Marital Pair Anger-coping Types May Act as an Entity to Affect Mortality: Preliminary Findings From a Prospective Study (Tecumseh, Michigan, 1971–1988)." *Journal of Family Communication* 8, no. 1 (2008): 44-61.

American Psychological Association. "Controlling Anger before It Controls You." *American Psychological Association.* http://www.apa.org/topics/anger/control.aspx (December 29, 2016).

2   Mostofsky, Elizabeth, Elizabeth Anne Penner, and Murray A. Mittleman. "Outbursts of Anger as a Trigger of Acute Cardiovascular Events: A Systematic Review and Meta-analysis." *European Heart Journal* 35, no. 21 (2014): 1404-1410.

3   Epstein, Robert, Ronald E. Robertson, Rachel Smith, Tyler Vasconcellos, and Megan Lao. "Which Relationship Skills Count Most? A Large-Scale Replication." *Journal of Couple & Relationship Therapy* 15, no. 4 (2016): 341-356.

4   van der Kolk, Bessel. *The Body Keeps the Score: Brain, Mind, and Body in the Healing of Trauma.* Reprint edition. London: Penguin Books, 2015.

5   Baikie, Karen A., and Kay Wilhelm. "Emotional and Physical Health Benefits of Expressive Writing." *Advances in Psychiatric Treatment* 11, no. 5 (2005): 338–46. doi:10.1192/apt.11.5.338.

6   Gottman, John M, and Nan Silver. *The Seven Principles for Making Marriage Work.* New York: Three Rivers

Press, 1999. Print.

7   Jensen, Jakob, Matthew Fish, Quianna Dinkins, Damon
      Rappleyea, and Katharine Didericksen. "Relationship
      Work Among Young Adult Couples: Romantic, Social,
      and Physiological Considerations." *Personal Relation-
      ships* 26, no. 2 (2019).

PART THREE:

FIXING GIANT PROBLEMS
(confronting the problem)

9. DAVID AND GOLIATH: THE TOOLS TO TEAM UP AGAINST PORN

It's not the size of the dog in the fight, it's the size of the fight in the dog.
  —Mark Twain

ADAM

I have something to confess: when I was about twelve years old, a bunch of neighborhood boys and I decided it would be a great idea to set up a sort of "fight club" in my backyard. It was summertime, we were all listless from sunny days with too much time on our hands, and I think we'd reached our quota of baseball card trades and daredevil bike stunts off plywood ramps.

So all the neighborhood kids gathered in my yard, and through some intricate selection process I can't recall, we paired them up to fight each other. The weird thing is, we were all friends. Nobody had any beefs with each other. We must have *really* been bored. I somehow avoided having to fight by securing myself a cushy administrative position. I've never been much of a fighter.

If you're reading this and wondering what on earth is wrong

with boys, I get it. If you have children, or plan to someday, and some of them are boys, please know that they'll probably turn out all right, even if they set up a fight club in your backyard on a hot summer day.

There was an unspoken rule in our fight club—and it wasn't "you do not talk about fight club." The rule was that fighters needed to be evenly matched. We never paired a huge kid with a small one or an older kid with a younger one. The fights needed to seem fair. Remember, we all wanted to stay friends afterward.

You have to know that when you take on porn, it's going to be a grudge match. It's not a fight between you and your partner. Remember, you two are a united front. Nope, this is a fight to the death between the two of you and porn. And it's not a fair fight.

If you're in a committed relationship and you've had The Talk, Wendy and I would recommend you read the rest of this book together with your partner. The degree to which he takes this process seriously will help you see how committed he is to both you and overcoming his porn use.

It's crucial for him to read with you because the information we'll present in the following chapters outlines for both of you the tools to achieve recovery. This will help you understand the steps your partner needs to take to beat this thing. But please know that his recovery is *not* your responsibility. It's his job alone to choose to use these tools.

We've also filled the following pages with plenty of life skills that will help you navigate your own experience and ensure your needs are met (including Chapter Fourteen that's devoted entirely to your well-being) as your partner works to recover from his compulsivity.

Now, why isn't the grudge match fair? The fact is, porn has a few shrewd assistants in its corner that help it fight dirty: dopamine, opioids, and novelty.

DOPAMINE AND OPIOIDS

WENDY

The neurotransmitter dopamine is a messenger that makes you

crave more of what you're doing. When you eat food or have sex, dopamine tells your body to keep eating to stay alive or have more sex to keep the species going. Opioids (not the class of drugs, but *endogenous opioids*, another type of neurotransmitter that exists naturally in your brain) make you feel relaxed, happy, and euphoric—communicating you must have just done the right thing, since you feel fantastic. Looking at porn gives people both a dopamine dump and a small but intense opioid dump into the reward pathway of their brains. That's part of the reason some people feel compelled to go back to porn again and again, even when they want to stop.

We mentioned back in Chapters One and Three that recent neuroimaging studies paint a revelatory picture about compulsive porn use. One such study revealed that when compulsive porn users are shown explicit videos, their brains display significantly greater sexual cravings than non-compulsive users and non-users, while at the same time they report *lower* enjoyment of the videos than the other study participants. This indicates they are becoming *habituated* to pornography—they want porn more than other people, but they actually like it less.[1]

NOVELTY

Porn also keeps your brain interested with the allure of novelty. [2] On the near-infinite internet, there's always a new erotic image or pornographic video awaiting discovery. Our brains are wired to crave and pay attention to new images and experiences.[3] As with sex and food, neuroimaging studies show that our brains also get a pleasant dopamine dump when we're exposed to something new. It can even be something as innocuous as viewing an "oddball" image after having watched a series of landscape photos. Our attraction to novelty may have given us an evolutionary advantage (a healthy sense of adventure no doubt helped us explore and populate the world, and our thirst to create the new likely spurred the tools and inventions necessary for survival).

In fact, novelty may be a crucial trait to having the best health, most friends, fewest emotional problems, and greatest life satisfaction, but only if it's tempered by two other key characteristics:

persistence (the ability to work toward something even when there's no immediate reward) and *self-transcendence* (feeling connected to nature and the universe as well as understanding that no, it's not all about you). But when novelty isn't paired with these two traits, it can lead to self-centered, antisocial behaviors.[4]

And the problem is, pornography use typically leads to disengagement more than persistent hard work, and it doesn't inspire a sense of wonder or consideration of others. Pure novelty seeking on its own is seldom helpful in our modern world where real, responsible adult life can seem quite mundane compared to the myriad escapes that screens provide. In Chapters Twelve and Thirteen, we'll talk more about how to access persistence and transcendence to balance the innate human drive to seek new experiences.

This double-reward of novelty and neurotransmitters does two things for a porn user: First, it gives him a compelling solution to boredom. Now, boredom may sound like an innocuous first-world problem. As a kid, when I made the mistake of complaining of boredom to my parents, the only real consequence that awaited me was a toilet to scrub.

But in recent years, behavioral scientists have turned their focus toward boredom and found that it affects more than privileged teenagers and has serious repercussions. Gambling, binge-eating, and other addictions and compulsive behaviors have been found to be linked with pervasive feelings of boredom.[5]

What's more, porn can create excitement in the porn user's brain that can help him numb emotional pain. It's natural to assume compulsive pornography use is about sex. But it isn't. At least, not in the way you might think. Like most compulsions, excessive porn use is often about coping with emotional pain. [6] People who excessively use porn and sex often suffer from underlying psychological disorders, such as depression, anxiety, and obsessive-compulsive disorder.[7] Acting out with pornography or other sexual behaviors becomes an outlet to escape pain.

ADAM

I see this in my office every day. Maybe there's a misconception out there about typical male porn users. Your average guy who is caught up with pornography isn't some creepy, greasy guy who dwells in the seedy underbelly of society. Your standard porn user is often a guy that you and I would both like. For the most part, I see well-meaning guys in my office who love their moms and are kind to animals, but who never learned to cope with the uncomfortable parts of life.

And usually, in an effort to quit, these guys try to exert all their willpower over their desire to use porn. It's obvious to them that porn use isn't doing them any good. Despite their best efforts to quit, they end up losing most of the time. Remember, this fight isn't fair. You can't conquer your own biology by just trying as hard as you can.

Because the fight isn't fair, a lot of guys I work with in therapy have felt pretty hopeless at some point. They worry they'll never end up quitting. But think of the stories where the underdog triumphs. Luke Skywalker and Darth Vader. Harry Potter and You-Know-Who. The shepherd boy David, who nobody thought could take on the nine-foot-tall monster Goliath and win.

Why do we love the underdog? Why do we turn again and again to the stories in which the unlikely hero defeats the odds and shows a supervillain who's boss?

We're drawn to those stories because they communicate an important truth: no matter how hopeless our predicament appears, no matter how formidable our opponent, he always has an Achilles heel. We always have a strength we didn't know we had, if only we can see with new eyes and find it.

So what are people missing, if sheer willpower isn't working? If your guy has gotten stuck in a never-ending battle with porn, how can he possibly conquer the porn-Goliath, when it uses his own brain against him? Well, let's start with evening the odds.

TAG-TEAM

First, we'll make this fight a tag-team match. Too many people can't overcome a pornography habit alone, no matter how much they might want to. If he's relied on his compulsions long enough, chances are they'll come back again, when the boredom, stress, or other painful emotions are high. I see people who try to quit alone, think they're making progress, and then fail repeatedly until they learn to enlist help. As a therapist, I can tell you that when people team up against pornography, good things start to happen.

But sometimes couples believe they've united against pornography when they don't yet have the tools that really work. Too often, women tell their partners, "I know you've looked at pornography in the past. Will you stop looking at it? And if you do look at it again, will you please come tell me?" And that's their entire plan, built on the unrealistic hope that porn will disappear. Unfortunately, it doesn't work. And this is what usually happens:

At some point, for any number of reasons, the partner slips back into using porn. And he's terrified. He knows how his wife feels about it. He's disappointed in himself. He has a moment of choice: confess or hide it. A guy who hides it often believes he's protecting his wife from pain. Or he knows he needs to tell her, but he just keeps waiting for the "perfect moment" that never comes. He might even rationalize that he can just wait to tell her at some point way off in the future, when he's overcome it on his own.

But whatever rationale he chooses, the shame of keeping this secret can suck him into watching even more porn as a coping mechanism. And because he's trying to do it on his own, he's not getting the help he needs. And the cycle continues.

So here's how we'll break that cycle: in order to bring you in as a tag-team partner in the grudge match, the two of you need to commit to *rigorous honesty*.[8] The more information you have about a problem, the more doable it becomes to conquer. You're going to continue being as honest as you were with each other during your first conversations about pornography, even when the truth is hard to hear. Rigorous honesty is telling the truth, exactly as it happened, with no attempt to control outcomes.

GET IT OUT INTO THE OPEN

The second way we'll level the playing field is by bringing pornography out into the open. Because porn is often taboo in our culture, we don't talk about it enough. Porn gets its power from people keeping it a secret out of shame and embarrassment.

Shame researcher Brené Brown has said that shame in a petri dish needs three things to grow: secrecy, silence, and judgment. [9] Secrets grow and grab hold of us. We spend unnecessary energy on the things we try to hide. And we get attached to the things we spend our energy on.

Porn draws its power from secrecy, a bit like the monster in a movie. The scariest movies avoid showing you the monster as long as they can. Until then, the movie survives on atmospheric eeriness. An old man warns the main characters that strange things happened in that house on the hill. Lights flicker. Pets act weird. Then the bizarre, unexplainable stuff starts to go down. People disappear in the woods. A rocking horse starts rocking all on its own. But the creature lurks just out of sight. And then, when you're almost at the action-packed ending, you *finally* get to see the monster that's been terrifying everybody for the previous ninety minutes.

And typically, whether it's some slimy beast with multiple sets of dagger-shaped teeth or a little girl with a mane of stringy hair and some crazy contortionist skills, seeing the monster is usually a bit of a letdown. It's never quite as bad as you imagined, and sometimes it feels a little goofy. It's the Wizard of Oz—not this giant, disembodied green head with a booming voice, but actually just some decrepit old dude standing behind a curtain, pulling a bunch of levers and talking into a microphone.

And that's how pornography is. It has more power when it's an illusion, when it lurks in the shadows because nobody wants to talk about it. Talking about pornography won't magically heal compulsive use, but getting the facts out in the open is the invaluable first step to recovery.

KNOWING WHAT WORKS: YOUR FIVE STONES

When David decided to fight Goliath, he first went to a dry riverbed and chose five smooth stones for his sling. They weren't anything out of the ordinary, but one of those stones killed the giant. Likewise, we'll give you a set of five ordinary-but-powerful tools to take down your own Goliath. They are simple adjustments to incorporate in your daily life. They won't seem like a magical fix.

But these stones are just what you need to punch porn between the eyes.

Anyone who has consistently watched pornography and tried to stop will tell you that there are plenty of tactics that don't work. Simply promising you won't do it again doesn't work. Trying to take up a hobby instead of porn doesn't work. Hoping that your newlywed sexual relationship will eliminate the compulsion to watch porn sadly won't work. Remember, a pornography habit isn't about sex, it's about emotional coping.

So let's talk about what does work. The following chapters will each focus on one of these small but effective stones in the fight against porn. First of all, you need to

SEEK SUPPORT

We've already talked about the importance of tag-teaming it. But you'll be able to draw additional strength from some carefully chosen helpers in your lives. They'll be there to get you through the toughest times. Chapter Ten will be all about the who, how, and why of bringing in reinforcements, the people you and your partner can lean on for extra help when you find you can't manage on your own.

MEET REAL NEEDS

I've said it before: compulsive porn use isn't all about sex. That's why an active sexual relationship doesn't cure it. Guys tend to start using porn out of curiosity. But they keep it up because it becomes a way for them to cope with difficult emotions, from pain to boredom to anxiety about the future. Most guys who can't quit porn have never learned to pay attention to their emotions.

A guy might *believe* he turns to porn for a sexual experience. But he has to learn that he doesn't know what he actually needs. Compulsive gamblers never feel better long-term by playing the slots (*even if they win*). Food addicts don't feel happy and fulfilled by food. Shopoholics never sit amidst their opulent piles of stuff and say, "I have now bought everything I will ever want. I have reached the pinnacle of existence. I am satisfied."

In order to overcome compulsive pornography use, a person needs to figure out their real needs, learn how to meet them when they can, and more importantly, learn to live with the discomfort when they can't be met right away.

BE ACCOUNTABLE

You know how you sometimes have this big project at work to accomplish or a research paper to write, and you put it off until the last possible second, and by that point you're frazzled and scrambling and doing an overall shoddy job? Why the heck do we do that to ourselves? Maybe we feel completely overwhelmed by the task. Maybe we're perfectionists, paralyzed by the fear that we'll do something wrong. Maybe the project is just plain boring.

Whatever the reason, for some of us, it's in our nature to do very little work unless we're being hounded by someone or something. Sometimes that little "push"—a deadline, an expectation—is all we need to get started or keep momentum. That's what accountability does for us. But that's not the only benefit of accountability.

Some of us don't need the push, but we all need accountability. Accountability is also seeing our actions through someone else's eyes so we can truly understand the ways our choices affect others. It's the humility to give up our will when we think we know better. It's also the mentorship that comes from listening to someone who's been there and has found a way out. In Chapter Twelve, we'll show you how accountability gets you on the road to recovery.

We'll also show you how to implement accountability into your relationship and why your partner can't be accountable to only you. Magic happens when he's accountable to someone who has been there, knows exactly how he's feeling, and has found their path to a porn-free life.

ACCESS MOTIVATION

The middle of a journey can be the hardest part. When you feel like you've been working your tail off, trying to take all of the steps, and you still haven't met your goal, it's easy to feel discouraged. We'll show you how motivation isn't just about getting what you want, and how that knowledge will help you get over any sticking points you have. We'll show you how to keep and grow your momentum, even when things seem to be going impossibly slow. We'll share secrets about how to use obstacles in your path to *improve* your motivation. And we'll help you budget your energy throughout the process of change to maximize the chances of long-term success.

TAKE CARE OF YOURSELF

And through all of this, you'll need to make sure your own needs are met. The women I see in my office who are involved with porn users are often loving, fiercely loyal, and "all in" when it comes to the fight against porn. In fact, one of the biggest problems I see among these women is that they're so committed to beat this thing that it becomes their sole focus in life. This struggle takes over their lives, and some can only be happy if their husband is abstaining from porn.

Tying your happiness to another person's choices, even your spouse's, is a recipe for unmitigated disaster. Too many of these women lose their sense of identity and see themselves exclusively as a partner of a recovering porn user. This chapter will be about how to maintain your own identity and manage to be emotionally stable and strong throughout the ups and downs.

So let's get to these tools so we can smack porn between the eyes.

GENEVIEVE   JULY 2007

The water's boiling when Genevieve arrives.
"Jake! Hey, Jacob! I'm home!"
No response.
"Did you want me to put in some pasta?"
She grabs a half-used package of spaghetti from the cupboard.
"JACOB?"

She breaks a stack of noodles in half and lets them fall into the water. Hopefully Jacob was planning on spaghetti. Then she makes the tiny trek into the front room, drops her keys, purse, and body onto the couch, putting her feet up on the coffee table, letting her eyes close for a few seconds.

Getting promoted to manager has been a godsend. She needs to remember that. At the end of each day, she's drained by every run between the stockroom, the aisles, and the checkout counter. Even more so with the long hours she has to take when employees flake out on their shifts. And she could do without having to referee the bickering between Debbie and Trent. And Debbie and Jean. And Debbie and Michael... Maybe Debbie's the problem.

No, it isn't quite the collegiate life she dreamed of. But she's got Jacob now. Everything's different. She'd always longed for a husband like him. And the five miles they put between Genevieve and her parents have given her space to breathe.

Genevieve sets her feet back down on the floor and opens the laptop on the coffee table, scouring the classified ads. There's a car wash in Baker City. Maybe they could buy that and run it from home together. Neither of them have owned a business before, but at least it would feel more stable than the grocery store. A job can always go away. Genevieve has managed to save a decent nest egg and keep it safe from her dad.

"Hey! I didn't hear you come in." Jacob sits down next to Genevieve. When she lifts her head, he kisses her lips.

She turns back to the computer. "I'm checking to see what businesses have come up for sale today. Here's a laundromat in Connecticut. We could manage something long-distance. If it was the right price."

Jacob grins at her.

"What?" she asks.

"I like your persistence."

"I'm excited to leave the grocery world behind me, okay? Interest rates are so low, it makes more sense to buy a business than to build one. I know I can do this. My dad once sunk a bunch of our money into an iPod app for dogs, so I know what *not* to do."

"We'll get there. You'll be amazing."

"Oh!" Genevieve sits up straight. "I put the spaghetti in. Are we doing spaghetti?"

"We are now," Jacob smiles, shrugging his shoulders.

Genevieve follows Jacob into the kitchen. He pulls a jar of sauce from the cupboard while she stirs the pot on the stove.

"So how's your paper coming?" she asks.

Jacob winces. "Well, you know. Not so great. I'm pretty overwhelmed. Every time I sit down to work on it, I don't even know where to start."

"But you're great at writing."

"Apparently not at business writing." Jacob shakes his head. "I miss my engineering classes, if you can believe that. This MBA program *might* be killing me, and this is just a prereq."

Genevieve opens her mouth to launch into her own crappy day but stops. Jacob's leaning forward up against the countertop, his arms supporting his entire weight. He looks blankly at his hands, like he's somewhere else.

"Jacob?"

He looks up at the cabinets, then breaks the silence. "Hey, so something happened at school today. I was in the library on my laptop. I was taking a break from writing the paper. That paper is killing me. I was, you know, messing around on the internet. So... I accidentally came across some pictures and, you know, some stuff I shouldn't have seen—like, pictures of girls."

Jacob's talking so fast, Genevieve has to replay what he just said in her mind to understand it.

"Anyway, I just thought I should tell you. But hey, you didn't tell me about your day yet. Any crazy Debbie stories?"

Genevieve stops stirring the sauce. "Wait, back up. What do you mean, 'pictures of girls'?"

Jacob gets quiet. "Well, you know, the internet is so sexualized. It's so hard to not see... you know... stuff."

Genevieve rubs her temples. "Do you mean, like, *porn*?"

Jacob mumbles, "Umm, yeah. I guess you could call it that."

"Oh, Jake. That happens." But her voice quivers. "You shut it down, though?"

"Yeah. Well..." Jacob looks pained.

Genevieve's stomach turns, "Jacob, what happened?"

Jacob looks down at his toes, scuffing at a mark on the floor with his shoe. "I didn't. Not for a while." He bites his bottom lip. "I don't know why I didn't stop. But I wasn't looking for it! I'll never do it again."

"Well, it was an accident..." Genevieve turns back to stirring the sauce.

"So how was your day?"

Genevieve turns back to Jacob again. "Wait—what *were* you looking for?"

"What?"

"Online. When you stumbled on the porn. What were you searching for?"

"I was just— I was just looking at... like, people."

"Looking at people? What does that mean?" Genevieve blinks. "Girls?? Were you looking for girls?"

Jacob's cheeks are pink. "Well, kind of. You know, I like to get ideas for characters, and writing fiction helps me get through the day."

Genevieve gives Jacob some serious side eye. "You were looking at girls to get ideas for characters?'

"Well, yeah."

"For a book?"

"Ummm... yeah."

The kitchen air is giving off the faintest stench of rotten fish.

"What book?"

"Well..." Jacob looks pained.

Genevieve's lion starts to roar. "I don't know what your problem is! And what do you mean you were taking a break from your paper? You just told me you haven't even started it!"

"No, I have. I just... Sometimes I need to take a break to clear my head."

"Take a break how?" Genevieve gasps. "*How many times has this happened?*"

Jacob flinches.

That tells her everything she needs to know. The room spins.

"Jenny, I came to you with this. You freaking out is making it worse."

"*What did you call me?*"

"Hey, why can't you just be nice to me?! I was trying to be honest!"

Genevieve suddenly feels hot and dizzy. She and Jacob have been married for *two months*. He'd had problems before, but they were having sex now. They were in love. He loved *her*. Right? Wasn't she enough for him?

Genevieve clenches her fists. "You sound like my dad! You're just making excuses!"

Genevieve can hear her voice, high and wild. And far away, like the words are coming from somebody else. She sees Jacob talking to her, but he looks so small right now. Things were supposed to be different with Jacob.

"You know what, Genevieve? Never mind! I'm sorry I brought it up!"

"No! I did not sign up for this!"

And before Genevieve can wonder what happened to the lovely newlywed dinner they were about to have, Jacob brushes past her toward the front door. He lets it slam behind him.

Hours later, when the door opens again, Genevieve is wide awake in bed. It's past midnight, but her racing mind won't let her escape to sleep. She hears him next to the bed.

"Genevieve?"

"I'm awake."

"Genevieve, I'm so, so sorry."

"Where did you go? You didn't take the keys or your phone."

"Just for a walk. To clear my head."

"For five hours?"

"There was a lot to clear. I promise I was just out walking."

Genevieve winces. She hates that he has to explain himself. She starts to say something, but for the second time today, she stops herself.

She tries again, "Jacob, I do love you. But this is not okay."

"I know. I know," he whispers. "I'm really, really sorry. I won't do it again."

Genevieve sighs. "I just didn't expect it. Not now. I thought things were going better."

"They *are*..." Jacob pauses. "They will. I promise."

Genevieve is quiet.

Jacob sits down on the bed. "You're the number-one most important person to me in the entire world. I don't know what I'd do if I screwed that up."

"*If* you screwed that up?"

"Okay, maybe I have screwed that up." Jacob's voice cracks. "I *have* screwed that up. But I'm going to make it right. I'll make it right, okay?"

Genevieve rolls over, toward Jacob. "Just come to bed. It's late."

Five minutes later, Jacob is in bed next to her, lying three feet away. He isn't holding her in his arms like he has every other night for the past two months. Genevieve takes a breath, then slides her hand over and touches him, resting two fingers on his arm. He gently pulls her in close. She can hear his heartbeat against her ear. But tonight Genevieve feels a little worn out, used up, empty. Everything seems different somehow. Like she's lost something she maybe never had.

1   Voon, Valerie, Thomas B. Mole, Paula Banca, Laura Porter, Laurel Morris, Simon Mitchell, Tatyana R. Lapa et al. "Neural Correlates of Sexual Cue Reactivity in Individuals With and Without Compulsive Sexual Behaviours." *PloS one* 9, no. 7 (2014): e102419.

2   Banca, Paula, Laurel S. Morris, Simon Mitchell, Neil A. Harrison, Marc N. Potenza, and Valerie Voon. "Novelty, Conditioning and Attentional Bias to Sexual Rewards." *Journal of Psychiatric Research* 72 (2016): 91-101.

3   Bunzeck, Nico, and Emrah Düzel. "Absolute Coding of Stimulus Novelty in the Human Substantia Nigra/VTA." *Neuron* 51, no. 3 (2006): 369-379.

4   Tierney, John. "What's New? Exuberance for Novelty Has Benefits." *The New York Times*, February 13, 2012. https://www.nytimes.com/2012/02/14/science/novelty-seeking-neophilia-can-be-a-predictor-of-well-being.html (accessed May 19, 2020).

5   Struk, Andriy. "Exploring the Relationship Between Self-regulation and Boredom." Master's thesis, (University of Waterloo, 2015).

6   Laier, Christian, and Matthias Brand. "Empirical Evidence and Theoretical Considerations on Factors Contributing to Cybersex Addiction From a Cognitive-Behavioral View." *Sexual Addiction & Compulsivity* 21, no. 4 (2014): 305-321.

7   Brand, Matthias, Christian Laier, Mirko Pawlikowski, Ulrich Schächtle, Tobias Schöler, and Christine Altstötter-Gleich. "Watching Pornographic Pictures on the Internet: Role of Sexual Arousal Ratings and Psycho-

logical-psychiatric Symptoms for Using Internet Sex Sites Excessively." *Cyberpsychology, Behavior, and Social Networking* 14, no. 6 (2011): 371-377.

Banca, Paula, Laurel S. Morris, Simon Mitchell, Neil A. Harrison, Marc N. Potenza, and Valerie Voon. "Novelty, Conditioning and Attentional Bias to Sexual Rewards." *Journal of Psychiatric Research* 72 (2016): 91-101.

8   Smith, Bob and Bill Wilson. *Alcoholics Anonymous: The Story of How Thousands of Men and Women Have Recovered From Alcoholism.* Fourth edition. New York: Alcoholics Anonymous World Services, Inc., 2001.

9   Brown, Brené. 2012. "Listening to Shame." March 2 in Long Beach, CA. TED video, 20:23, https://www.ted.com/talks/brene_brown_listening_to_shame (accessed June 21, 2021).

10. STONE #1: SEEKING SUPPORT

If you want to go quickly, go alone; if you want to go far, go together.
  —possibly an African proverb, definitely a quote by former Vice President Al Gore

ADAM

We all have strengths. But no one has all the strengths. In my therapy practice, I often hear this story from guys who are working through a porn problem: "I tried for years to fix it on my own. Nothing I tried ever worked. I eventually realized that I couldn't do it myself. When I finally got help, things started to change."

I understand their stubbornness and fears about reaching out. I've avoided getting help for some of the most ridiculous things (i.e., learning how to change diapers) to my own detriment—sometimes because I didn't want to burden anyone, and at other times because I was afraid to admit I was clueless. Eventually, most of us realize we're all in this together. Life is much happier and more productive when we stop pretending we don't need anyone.

WENDY

Communication guru Matt Townsend has a lot to say about why people go farther together. In fact, he would argue that we can even go *faster* together. Like Adam, Matt helps people build outstanding relationships and marriages. He's a jolly, round-faced man, equal parts stand-up comedian and wise sage.

At Townsend's crowd-drawing lectures, he often begins by explaining the seemingly magical concept of *draft*,[1] a phenomenon among competitive cyclists. Have you ever wondered why cyclists travel together in tight groups during races, sometimes mere inches apart, so close they appear to be in danger of crashing into each other? It's because the closer they are, the stronger the draft they create.

Draft is a vortex in the space between two or more cyclists, and it allows them to travel faster than they would alone. Both the cyclists at the back *and* the cyclists in the lead benefit from draft. Together, they can expend up to forty percent (!) less energy in their travels and arrive at the finish line faster than they would by themselves.[2] Draft is the reason that finish times in pairs cycling (in which two cyclists ride together) are consistently lower than in single races.

Townsend explains that the magic of draft doesn't come from the cyclist in the back or the one in the front. It actually comes from the space between them. The essence of this chapter is drawing on that powerful space between you, your partner, and everyone else in your support system.

ADAM

In order to get in on the magic of draft, you'll have the option to enlist three types of support:

1. Friends and family members you can trust and confide in.
2. A structured support community (like twelve-step or other recovery groups), with people who've been where you are now.

3. A qualified therapist or expert mentor, preferably one who specializes in treating problematic sexual behavior.

As you two discuss who to seek help from, you and your future husband will likely have some differing opinions. And coming up with a plan may take awhile. Create the support system that works for you. Finding support is not a simple, one-size-fits-all solution, and it may involve some trial and error. That's okay.

Asking for help may end up being more difficult for him than for you. It's not easy to admit to having a compulsion that many people assign a strong value judgment to. Both of you will need to access some bravery to find the support you need. Remember, trying to get better on your own is the risky choice. Don't be the lone cyclist trying to win the pairs race.

WENDY

The reality is that the road to healing may be longer than you'd like, as in the case of a woman named Monica. Listening to her story, I wondered if other people with the same experience might have thrown in the towel. But Monica's a fighter. Bold and confident, a physician's assistant, piano teacher, and a mom of three daughters, Monica is no slouch at life.

Ten years ago, Monica thought she was living the good life with a faithful, loving husband and a growing family. That all changed one Saturday night when her husband Christian was away on a business trip. Monica had just put her wiggly toddler to bed and planned on taking the next hour to prepare a lesson for the children's class she would teach at church the following day. Monica's church had always been a place of refuge and belonging for her, so she didn't mind doing her part to help out, even though she was eight months pregnant with her second child.

As always seems to be the case when you need to get something done ASAP, Monica's computer crashed before she was done writing her lesson plan. So Monica grabbed Christian's laptop to finish up. She seldom touched Christian's computer, but desperate times called for desperate measures. She booted up his computer, and just like that, there was the porn—years of secrets Christian had kept from Monica.

She was devastated, and she didn't understand. But she had to wait three days until Christian came home. She wanted to confront him face to face. When she did, Christian broke down and admitted to everything. Monica could tell that he hated himself for using porn and lying to his wife. As heartbroken as Monica was, she was determined to get them help. This would just be a bump in the road, she decided.

It was more than a bump. Over the next few years, Monica and Christian tried everything. They met with the pastor of their congregation, who was well-meaning but tried to shame Christian into abstinence. They attended couples counseling with a therapist who had no idea how to heal a pornography habit. None of it seemed to help. Christian couldn't white knuckle very long without turning to porn.

As the years passed and Christian wasn't getting any better, Monica felt increasingly distant from her faith community. At the church that used to be her sanctuary, Monica now felt like an outsider. In Monica's eyes, everyone at church seemed to live these squeaky-clean lives. She didn't believe they could possibly understand what she was going through.

Monica had confided in her sister, who was understanding but also a busy mom who lived nearly a thousand miles away. They didn't get to talk very much. Christian's three brothers were all compulsive porn users too, but the entire family just ignored the problems, their heads in the sand in shame. Monica's father-in-law was a high-ranking religious leader in their denomination, and the double lives the sons led were too much for anyone in that family to process.

Monica eventually found a tiny bit of solace in a support group for partners of porn users that met once a week. Four other women of her faith attended the group. "But we were all drowning," Monica relates. "Their happiness was tied to their husbands' sobriety, and so was mine." No one could show them how to find healing for themselves. But at least Monica had people to commiserate with every Tuesday night.

Even still, as the years passed with no improvement for Christian, a fatalistic depression wrapped its tendrils around Monica's life. She began to believe that with nothing changing, she and Christian were doomed. She didn't know then that happiness was waiting for her, years down the road.

FRIENDS AND FAMILY

ADAM

Under the right circumstances, seeking support from people in your personal life who love both of you can be incredibly healing. It can help you ward off the crushing loneliness and isolation that often come from trying to conquer porn on your own. The loneliness Monica felt during those dark years isn't limited to her story. In Chapter Three, we discussed how common it is for women married to pornography users to experience it.[3]

That said, you're not just going to ask the whole village for help in this case. You're not looking for the sympathy of everyone you know. You want to balance your partner's need for respect and privacy with the need you both have for support.

We've all met some people who overshare. It usually doesn't go too well for them socially. You know who I'm talking about—the cashier at the grocery store you've never even met before who, entirely unprompted, shares the epic tale of her divorce, including how she's *still fuming* that Jim took the dog, when you just want to pay for your gallon of milk. Or that uncle you see once a year at Thanksgiving, who walks in the house, gives you a big hug, and starts giving you the gory details of his irritable bowel syndrome.

We don't want you to shapeshift into one of those people because then you won't be invited to parties. Seeking support in this sense doesn't mean airing all your private grievances on social media for your coworkers, elementary school friends, and Aunt Brenda to weigh in on. Remember, your future husband likely doesn't want you to broadcast the story of his pornography use to the entire planet.

WENDY

Research supports being very careful about what and whom you share with. In one study of women in their twenties in committed relationships, researchers found that when women discussed relationship problems with an outside party like their best friend, they increased their odds of breaking up by thirty-three percent. But women who talked out their relationship problems with their significant others rather than a friend were twice as likely to be together by the end of the study.[4]

Confide in each other first, before you turn to anyone else. And having outside support to lean on isn't about having someone to take your side while you vent all your frustrations. You want to share with people who care about both of you and want to see you succeed as a team. When you do look to others to lean on, be very careful about who you choose to share with.

In fact, many of the individuals I interviewed didn't have anyone in their personal lives that they could trust to understand and support them through their battle with a porn habit. For some, their loved ones were too biased against porn use to believe the couple should stick with the relationship. For others, their friends' and families' distress about pornography caused more harm than good. These couples ended up finding much-needed emotional support from people they met in their twelve-step groups. The relationships people form in these groups are often the most raw, close, and honest they've ever had, which we'll discuss further in the section on support groups.

HOW TO CHOOSE HELPERS FROM YOUR FRIENDS AND FAMILY

ADAM

When choosing someone to confide in, look for someone in your life who cares about both of you and who you believe to be open-minded, trustworthy, and helpful. Choose someone who is

- Invested in both of your well-being
- Emotionally stable and predictable
- Able to provide support without placing blame
- Reasonably available to you
- Willing to listen to and hold space for you, without feeling like they need to advise you or fix your problem

But above all,

- Trust your gut.

You might be tempted to rush to tell your parents about your partner's problems the moment you find out about them. Here's the issue: you're trying to develop a relationship that's separate from your parents. And while your parents may mean well, they'll usually be more invested in protecting you from pain than helping you nurture your relationship. This doesn't mean you should never talk to your parents about what you're both going through. I'm simply saying that you need to be careful about if, when, and how you do it.

Optimally, the two of you will sit down together and decide how you would like to seek support from people who love you. Discuss the relative merits of each possible helper. Whatever you decide, if you make up your minds together, it will turn out better.

At the same time, life is rarely optimal. Maybe your partner demands that you not share his story with anyone. Maybe he refuses to let you even consider seeking help. When this happens, it usually means he still feels deep shame about his compulsions. You love him and want to respect his privacy, but you're torn because it doesn't feel fair to have no one to turn to.

Be mindful of your own needs, and balance them with the needs of your developing relationship. Tell your partner that you understand his need for privacy. Honor that need. And share your need to not struggle in silence. Help him see that your mental health will fare better if the two of you have some people in your corner. And have that conversation as many times as it takes to find some common ground and a solution that both of you feel comfortable with. You'll both be negotiating your respective needs for the rest of your life. That's just part of marriage.

Again, trust your gut. Don't go behind your partner's back, but do what feels right in the moment. Every decision has consequences, but if your relationship is worth hanging onto, the two of you will be able to overcome the challenges that come from difficult choices.

WHAT TYPE OF SUPPORT TO EXPECT FROM FRIENDS AND FAMILY

Your loved ones won't likely be recovery or healing experts. Most of the time, they won't even know what to say when you're sharing the pain of your soul. They don't need to advise you, and you can tell them that (since it's human nature to want to fix each other's problems). Their job is to care about the two of you. You simply need to know that, regardless of how your relationship turns out, they will still love and support you and be ready to listen when you need to vent or share your burden. Sometimes we just need to know that somebody cares.

Leave the advice and the structure to the next two groups of helpers that we'll discuss below. Let your close family and friends remind you that no matter what happens, some people will always have your back.

And if you don't have healthy family or friends to rely on right now, you'll be grateful to find some amazing friends and helpers in recovery support groups.

SUPPORT GROUPS

We humans need each other. "The human brain is wired for close connection,"[5] writes Dr. Sue Johnson, one of the foremost experts on human relationships. Furthermore, we often fare better with a little framework and planning, rather than flying through life by the seat of our pants.

Both of those facts may be why twelve-step programs often play a big role in my clients' recovery from porn. In 1934, an alcoholic named Bill Wilson found freedom from the grip of alcoholism— with God's help, by his account. Whether by divine or human origins, Alcoholics Anonymous (AA), the founding twelve-step program, was born. Those who fully invest in AA and its mission will tell you that those twelve-step meetings, having a sponsor, and "working the steps" are the only things that really made any difference for them in their quest for recovery.

And twelve-step programs are no longer limited to alcoholism. Today, twelve-step groups help people recover from all sorts of addictions, from drugs, to gambling, shopping, gaming, or food. And porn.

WENDY

Monica's story didn't end with that first support group. Years after believing help would never come, Monica found a program that offered group therapy in addition to individual and couples counseling. It was expensive, but Monica had just received a $2000 check from her grandfather, and she knew how she wanted to use it.

This time, all forms of therapy targeted compulsive pornography use, which meant Christian met men with struggles similar to his own. "For the first time in his life, he started to think, 'Maybe I'm not a monster; I'm just a person with a lot of shame,'" Monica told me. That wasn't the end of Christian's porn use, but it was his first step to understanding what was fueling his compulsions.

Unfortunately, the group Monica attended with other women wasn't any better than the last one. There were ten women this time, but again, they were all drowning in unhealed trauma. No one knew how to find healing independent of their husband's porn use. And eventually, the money ran out for Monica and Christian's therapy/support group. Years passed.

But then one night, Monica found herself sitting in her car outside of an entirely different church, forty minutes from her home in Texas, nervous but determined. She had read online about a free twelve-step program for partners of sex addicts. She understood she would likely meet women whose partners' indiscretions had moved far beyond porn, a thought which made her squirm. But she took a deep breath and went inside.

About fifteen women sat in a circle on folding chairs. Monica would soon come to find out that, yes, their partners' sexual behaviors involved much more than screens. But what surprised Monica most at that meeting was the atmosphere in the room. The women were smiling and laughing. They spoke about finding peace. It felt more like a party among old friends than a place to gather and crumble in despair, hoping in vain someone might be there to catch you. Monica exhaled, not realizing how much she'd longed to laugh and smile again herself.

Monica would soon learn that two-thirds of the women at that meeting had found recovery from their trauma, some for many years.

Among this unlikely group of friends, Monica finally saw that peace was possible. "These ladies—some of their husbands had been *in jail*. They'd done *way* more than what Christian had. But they were happy people." Maybe there was life after a husband's porn habit.

Monica kept making those forty-minute drives for the next year, continually amazed by it all. In the other recovery groups she'd attended, the women's job was to support their husbands in their step work. But this was the first place she'd seen women working the twelve steps for *themselves*. They were seeking their own serenity from their traumas and troubles.

But Monica still didn't understand, she told me. She's a woman who's used to being in charge in all areas of her life. She had no idea what it meant to surrender everything to her higher power. Christian was still actively using pornography. Could she really be happy when he wasn't sober? She resigned herself to nothing really changing, glad to at least be around women who had their lives back, and grateful for a sponsor to call when the darkness started to close in.

But then, about a year after Monica attended that first meeting, when she'd learned to be more or less content with her discontent, something changed. Even today, Monica herself doesn't quite understand it. She calls it a miracle. She says that after years of trying to find peace, she finally had enough faith to surrender.

"And it happened," she tells me. "It was like magic. And maybe it has worked differently for other people, but I had to learn to surrender from those women whose husbands had been in similar or worse situations than mine. Because someone at church, whose life seems perfect, telling me to surrender—I would just think, *You don't even know what you're talking about.*"

At long last and in an instant, Monica was at peace, regardless of her husband's choices. She had found salvation among some unexpected and supportive friends.

ADAM

I believe there are as many paths to healing and recovery as there are people. In some ways, your path will look different than anyone else's. But I also can't deny what plays out in my therapy office: my clients who fully invest in a healing community are so much more likely to "get better" than those who are isolated and try to do it on their own. In most cases, these clients are attending one of various free and anonymous sex addiction recovery groups, like Sexaholics Anonymous or Sex Addicts Anonymous.

But please note: it's not your job to convince your partner to attend a recovery group. He has to decide if a healing community is right for him. But you can be proactive about your own healing by attending a support group for partners, like S-Anon. These meetings are for family members and other loved ones of people who struggle with sexual compulsivity. These meetings will help you learn to let go of his choices, work toward your own personal healing, and support your partner if you choose to, without getting sucked into the "rescuer" role.

There are plenty of books out there to help you understand the scope and benefits of twelve-step programs. We've listed some for you in Appendix C. But let me just tell you that many of my clients find twelve-step programs, with their focus on surrender and the healing companionship of sponsors, invaluable for their recovery.

Russell Brand, an unlikely poster boy for twelve-step with his coarse humor and out-of-control past, shares some potent truths about the allure of compulsions and the power the twelve steps wield to free you: "The instinct that drives compulsion is universal. It is an attempt to solve the problem of disconnection, alienation, tepid despair... the problem is ultimately 'being human' in an environment that is curiously ill-equipped to deal with the challenges that entails."[6]

The twelve steps teach you to find your humanity, to build real connection and hope instead of turning to an empty solution that will never satisfy you.

While attending the meetings is valuable, recovery truly begins when you work the twelve steps, which is best done with the help of a sponsor. Working the steps isn't something you accomplish on your own with a workbook in hand—you need someone who's been down the path you're on and can guide your journey. A sponsor can help you get traction for change. They've earned wisdom from years of experience in their own recovery program. They keep you accountable, and because they've been where you or your partner are, they might understand this part of you better than anyone.

Monica found hope and direction when she finally could see with her own eyes what recovery looks like, and when she had someone to call who could support her and remind her to surrender. Sponsors provide their own "experience, strength, and hope"[7] regarding recovery, and they're always a phone call away. Even better, most sponsors will offer their unfiltered opinion about why you may be stuck.

And because recovery is so personal, most sponsors won't dictate your journey. They'll share what's worked for them and help you find insight into what may work for you. But their raw feedback may be a breath of fresh air for those who want rigorous honesty about finding recovery. As far as a cycling buddy goes, it's hard to do better than a good twelve-step sponsor. Because so many people find sponsors integral to their recovery, we'll give you more information about sponsors in Chapter Twelve.

A SPECIALIZED THERAPIST OR EXPERT MENTOR

WENDY

Two years passed. Monica's recovery was strong, but Christian was stagnating, stuck in his compulsive porn use. He'd lost interest in even trying. When Monica took the kids to stay with family in California without Christian, she told him she wasn't certain when or if she would come back, because she truly didn't know. A few weeks later, when Monica couldn't shake a nagging feeling that she needed to come home, she made the drive back.

She was shocked to find a Christian she'd never met before. Monica had always been the engineer of the recovery train in their marriage, but this time Christian had enrolled in a twelve-step program in Monica's absence. Soon after, he found a therapist who worked for him. A tough, no-nonsense lady with specialized training in sexual compulsivity, she was just what Christian needed to engage sobriety and take the true steps toward recovery. This blunt, intimidating, ultra-qualified therapist, who had no time to worry about whether or not Christian felt like they were friends, just happened to have the formula Christian needed to start making progress.

As for Monica, she found the final piece of her healing puzzle in front of a computer screen, drawing strength from other women who "got" her in every way. Grateful as she was for the relationships she'd built with the women from her most recent support group, Monica still longed to connect with people of her own faith. She didn't want to feel alone in a place she had called home since she was a little girl. "I needed connection with someone who believes what I believe, but who can also understand and bear this *huge* part of my life."

And that's what the online twelve-step meetings brought her. Part of a nondenominational program, but founded by and filled with many people of her own faith, they work steps. They focus on sponsors and phone calls. They are just the support community Monica needs. Although Monica still feels misunderstood at church sometimes, she can get on her computer each week and talk to women scattered all over the globe who have lived her life and know her struggles. "They make me feel like I'm not a loser for having a husband who is a porn addict," she tells me.

Monica needed women who understood, and Christian needed a qualified therapist whose approach worked for him. Christian's story is one I heard again and again in different words throughout the interviews. Nearly every person I spoke to at one point sought therapy from a practitioner who was largely unacquainted with the principles of recovery from porn use—sadly, to disastrous results. Edwin's first therapist, who didn't have specific training in treating compulsive sexual behaviors, only treated him for social anxiety, missing the potential link between his porn use and his anxiety. The same was true for a porn user I interviewed named Luke, but this therapist only treated his depression and ignored his porn problem. For another couple, a therapist early in their marriage told the wife to issue ultimatums in order to get results and leave her husband for good if he ever relapsed, even though ultimatums seldom work with compulsions, and neither of them wanted to break up.

But I also heard plenty of stories of the value of seeing a therapist who spends all of her time treating and understanding these specific issues. The same individuals who started off on the wrong foot with a general therapist eventually found therapists who specialized in treating compulsive sexual behaviors and understood their effects on relationships. I heard resounding "yeses" when I asked these couples if specialized therapy was helpful. Most of them cite therapy as integral to their healing.

ADAM

In your search for a great therapist, look for raw honesty, experience, and specialization. In medicine, general practitioners are great for head colds, weird pains, or pulled muscles. But you wouldn't see your GP for a cancer diagnosis. You'd visit an oncologist. You want someone who does pretty much one thing—and hopefully does it well. If I were in your shoes, I'd make a bunch of phone calls. I'd call four or five therapists, or more if I had to, until I found someone who seemed like they knew exactly what they were talking about. Someone who was extremely focused on this treatment area.

While seeing a therapist who's wrong for you can be less than helpful, there is great benefit in receiving feedback from the right one. The best therapists can help you formulate a personalized game plan. Not only that, but if a person with unhealthy coping behaviors has unresolved childhood trauma that contributes to their compulsions, a therapist will help them address that trauma. That was the case with a compulsive porn user named Danny, who we'll see more of in Chapter Twelve. Part of his recovery included working through his childhood trauma, which is beyond the scope of a spiritually oriented twelve-step program. Compulsive porn users often suffer from other underlying issues that may be fueling their compulsion, from depression to social anxiety to paranoid thinking. Therapy can be invaluable in helping someone understand and confront the issues driving their compulsive behavior.[8]

A therapist will also be specially trained to listen to you and understand you in ways other people in your life may not be.

A good therapist is worth their weight in a briefcase full of unmarked, non-sequential hundred dollar bills. A therapist can provide honest feedback, an expert perspective, compassionate understanding, and help bypassing your own mental defenses to help you get unstuck when all of your best efforts seem to be getting you nowhere. I'm definitely biased, considering my profession, but therapy is great.

Unfortunately, not everyone lives near a great therapist. I know lots of people who live in rural areas or small cities, where finding a therapist isn't an easy task. Or you may not even want to see a professional or might have other reasons why that path just isn't for you.

It may take some hunting, but there are options out there for expert mentors, coaches, or other specialized helpers that focus on compulsive sexual behaviors or pornography use. The internet is your friend. In a post-COVID world, you'll also find online-only choices that offer high-quality service. Do your homework and try out some options.

You may not *need* an expert professional by your side, but when you do, take your search seriously. The wealth of knowledge and experience of a trained professional is invaluable.

You don't have to wait for your partner to decide to seek help, either. You can attend therapy for yourself if your future husband isn't ready. Your experience is just as important as his in this process, and talking with an expert may be just what you need to get clarity about which steps to take for your personal and relational health.

WENDY

Monica and Christian finally found the feedback and help they each needed. Are they living in their "happily ever after" of complete recovery? Not yet. Like most of us, they're still in the middle of their story, hoping for a happy ending. Monica has given Christian a list of changes she needs to see in order to feel safe fully investing in her marriage. He's achieved most of them. One item is three months of sobriety, more than he's ever had in their entire married life, a goal which he has long surpassed now. Monica says that now Christian almost always acknowledges when he's feeling anger or shame and surrenders his emotions. They're both working hard to build a loving, healed relationship.

And gritty Monica has traveled *miles* from where she was. "I feel..." And then she pauses, like she's hoping in vain to hold back tears. "I *can't* tell you how grateful I am to not be in that place anymore. And I don't ever have to go back to it, regardless of my husband. I'm not in trauma anymore," she explains. "I was, but it's gone now."

She's telling the truth. I've interviewed women in trauma, seen their struggle to remember events, watched how they recoil almost reflexively at questions that seem ordinary. Monica is none of those things. Monica is calm and present as she tells her story. "I would never have said this ten years ago, but I'm actually glad Christian and I have experienced what we did, because it made me into the person I need to be." The darkness and isolation of Monica's struggle compelled her to find the team she needed to be able to draft her way to healing and grow further than she ever could have on her own.

Jacob startles awake when Genevieve, cell phone pressed to her ear, places a tiny pile of moving limbs and warm, damp breath in his lap. Jacob sits up and pulls the baby close, hugging her tight to his chest as he yawns and stretches, then rubs the sore left side of his forehead, indented from the corner of his desk. He moves the mouse to bring the monitor to life.

5:03 PM. Almost two whole hours lost to sleep. His stomach churns as he looks over the measly twenty-two pages he's written of his capstone project, due in less than a week.

Genevieve's shaky voice drifts through the air as she leaves the tiny second bedroom they use for an office and now a nursery. But she isn't talking to Jacob.

"Mom... Mom. Yeah, I hope you finally get your diagnosis... Uh-huh..."

Shoulders slumped, she paces up and down the hallway outside the door. "Hey, Mom... Mom! What was the name of the baby monitor you had for Mara? The one with three speakers for different rooms?"

Jacob saves his file, opens his browser, and Googles "baby monitor with three speakers." He finds a baby supply site that lists a system with three video monitors instead of speakers. Even better. Free shipping. Perfect. Genevieve won't have to run into the baby's room at all hours of the night to make sure she's still alive. When Genevieve paces past the doorway again, he waves at her with his free hand. She doesn't see him.

"No, Mom, we can't go to that. We're so tired... Just tell them we can't come."

It even doubles as a carbon monoxide detector. She'll love it. Jacob calls her name as she passes.

She looks over at Jacob and puts an index finger in the air. Just a second. Okay. "Yes, Mom, I know it's hard for you to get out too...

Yes, I know you had babies too! What are you trying to say, Mom?"

Jacob's jaw tightens. The baby brings her fists up over her head and lets out a tiny cry. Is she hungry? When Genevieve paces to the back of the hallway, he makes his move for the kitchen. He grabs a vial of breast milk from the fridge and puts it in a mug of hot water. He bounces the baby as the milk warms. He puts the milk in a bottle and brings it up to her mouth. She opens her mouth for a second, then turns her head away.

"What are you doing?!" Genevieve is standing in the kitchen doorway. She sets the phone down on the side table they use as a kitchen desk. Now she has time for him.

"She was crying. I thought she was hungry."

"She just nursed twenty minutes ago!"

"I didn't know that!"

"Yeah, 'cause you were asleep."

"I was trying to finish my project. I'm tired, okay?"

"Do you think I'm not tired? My body gave birth less than two months ago. And I have to go back to work next week, and we don't have any money. And you just wasted an entire bottle of breastmilk. We can't reheat it again."

"It would be fine if we reheated it. Those baby books are just trying to scare us."

"Jacob! That introduces bacteria! I am not feeding my baby bacteria!" Genevieve sighs and shakes her head, slumping onto the couch. "That was like twenty minutes of pumping down the drain."

"Well, I tried to talk to you, but you were on the phone with your mom. Why do you even call her? You're always miserable afterward!"

Genevieve rolls her eyes and stands back up, her face pink. "Agggh! What kind of question is that? She's my mom! She called me! What was I supposed to do? Ignore her? Disown her?"

Jacob's stomach flip-flops.

Genevieve clenches her jaw. "And I was trying to get help for *our* baby."

Jacob remembers and makes a run for the office, still cradling the baby in the crook of his arm. "Oh! I found something!"

Genevieve follows him, her footsteps slow. "What?"

When she reaches the office, Jacob pulls out the chair for her and wiggles the mouse again. She folds her arms, eyes Jacob sideways, then sits.

"Here! Look—it's a video monitor with three outputs, so we can see from the bed if Maya's awake and safe. Or the couch. Or the kitchen."

Jacob leans over the chair to look at Genevieve's face. But she isn't smiling. "Jake, we can't afford this. We need to find a used monitor. Without video."

She looks away. She's still wearing the pajama pants she slept in last night—if she got any sleep. Her hair, grown out to her chin now, points every which way, defying gravity.

She gets up and turns to Jacob with sagging eyes. "Thanks for trying to help." She sighs, resting her hand on his forearm for a few seconds before she walks out of the room, but he barely feels it.

The room is quiet now. Failure has dampened the pulsing heat of the argument.

Of course they can't afford it. He was supposed to be Mr. Frugality for Genevieve. If he could just do one nice thing for her... He owes her that. He owes her a whole lot more than that.

Jacob sits down at the computer. He closes the browser and sees the wallpaper on their monitor. Genevieve looking like an angel in her white dress and Jacob with his arms around her waist, facing her as if she's the only thing in his world. He remembers that day, over two years ago, back when he could hardly believe so much happiness was meant for him. Or those times after they moved into this place, when they found themselves standing close to each other in this tiny room. The times they couldn't keep their hands off each other.

Or the night Jacob sat at this computer and Genevieve yelled from the bathroom across the hall, her voice trembling, that he was going to be a dad. Jacob felt like a kid himself that day. But also like he and Genevieve now shared some miracle together.

But too many of Jacob's secrets have built up like a wall between them, putting him on edge. Sometimes he snaps at Genevieve about the dishes in the sink, the baby crying, nothing whatsoever, when his secrets are darker than any ordinary flaws Genevieve may have. All the hours he wastes on campus, with nothing to show for his time away from his wife and daughter. Secretly breaking Genevieve's heart without having the decency to let her know. Clicking through infinite porn sites at school or late at night when he should be taking care of all of them. He can hardly breathe through the secrets.

Maya's hand brushes over his. She looks up at him, giving him a half smile when her eyes rest on his face. He points with his index finger beneath her palm, and she wraps her tiny fingers around it, as if he's all she needs in this world.

Jacob clicks back to his project. He's got half an intro and the first chapter written. Under the dread of looming deadlines, a cold lump grows in Jacob's stomach. It will all come crashing down soon enough. Genevieve and Maya will leave, and that will be the end. Because why would a girl like her stay with a liar like him?

1   Townsend, Matt. "Power Up: Foster Fantastic Relation-
     ships with Clients (and in Your Marriage)" Breakout pre-
     sentation, Keller Williams Family Reunion, Las Vegas,
     February 2017.

2   Doherty, Paul. "Drafting." *The Science of Cycling*.
     exploratorium.edu/cycling/aerodynamics2 (accessed
     November 5, 2019).

3   Bergner, Raymond M., and Ana J. Bridges. "The Signifi-
     cance of Heavy Pornography Involvement for Romantic
     partners: Research and Clinical Implications." *Journal of
     Sex & Marital Therapy* 28, no. 3 (2002): 193-206.

4   Jensen, Jakob, Matthew Fish, Quianna Dinkins, Damon
     Rappleyea, and Katharine Didericksen. "Relationship
     Work Among Young Adult Couples: Romantic, Social,
     and Physiological Considerations." *Personal Relation-
     ships* 26, no. 2 (2019).

5   Johnson, Susan. "Ten Tips for a Strong, Vibrant Relation-
     ship." Dr. Sue Johnson: Creating Connections. drsue-
     johnson.com/ten-tips-for-a-strong-vibrant-relationship
     (accessed August 3, 2019.)

6   Brand, Russell. *Recovery: Freedom from our Addictions*.
     New York: Henry Holt and Co., 2017.

7   Smith, Bob and Bill Wilson. *Alcoholics Anonymous:
     The Story of How Thousands of Men and Women Have
     Recovered From Alcoholism*. Fourth edition. New York:
     Alcoholics Anonymous World Services, Inc., 2001.

8   Brand, Matthias, Christian Laier, Mirko Pawlikowski,
     Ulrich Schächtle, Tobias Schöler, and Christine Alt-

stötter-Gleich. "Watching Pornographic Pictures on the Internet: Role of Sexual Arousal Ratings and Psychological-psychiatric Symptoms for Using Internet Sex Sites Excessively." *Cyberpsychology, Behavior, and Social Networking* 14, no. 6 (2011): 371-377.

11. STONE #2:
MEETING REAL NEEDS

To feel intensely is not a symptom of weakness, it is the trademark of the truly alive and compassionate.
—Anthon St. Maarten

ADAM

If you were lost in the desert, parched and dehydrated, and I offered you, say, a bottle of vinegar to drink, what would you do? If you'd gone long enough without water, I bet you'd pucker up and drink it. Of course, your body would be screaming for some ice-cold H_2O. But beggars can't be choosers, as they say.

Most people with a history of pornography use believe they just want more sexual experiences. Then they're confused to find that the porn use doesn't magically go away once they're in a committed sexual relationship. I'm sorry to say I've seen scores of couples who thought marriage would cure their pesky porn problem. They still ended up in my office.

What these couples don't know is that compulsive pornography use is seldom about sex; it's about unmet needs. Porn users are chugging vinegar, and often they don't even know that they're dying of thirst. In order to have full relationships and lives, these beggars need to learn to choose water.

MASLOW AND MOSQUITOES

WENDY

Using porn to try to meet your needs is a lot like scratching a mosquito bite. It may alleviate the itch for a moment, but the irritation will soon return with a vengeance. Do you know why scratching a mosquito bite makes it worse?

The gory details: We're allergic to a mosquito's saliva, which it squirts into the wound. Your body responds by sending histamines to the site, causing the bite to become irritated, begging to be scratched. This begins what dermatologists like to call the "itch-and-scratch cycle." When you scratch a mosquito bite, you experience temporary relief, emphasis on *temporary*. Scratching a mosquito bite only sends more histamines, increasing the inflammation, which makes the area itch *more* after a minute or two. Plus, scratching a bite can introduce dirt and bacteria into the region, which may cause an infection that makes the bite take longer to heal. A moment of soothing comes at a cost, increasing the itch with time and prolonging healing. Sound familiar?

Scratching the itch always makes it worse. Unfortunately, knowing that isn't enough to solve your problem. When an itch is driving us bonkers, we might intellectually understand that our body just needs to follow its own protocol to heal. But how often do we ignore our body's needs and scratch the itch anyway?

Abraham Maslow is The Guy when it comes to human needs. He developed a hierarchy with our most basic survival necessities represented at the bottom and our need to contribute to society at the top:

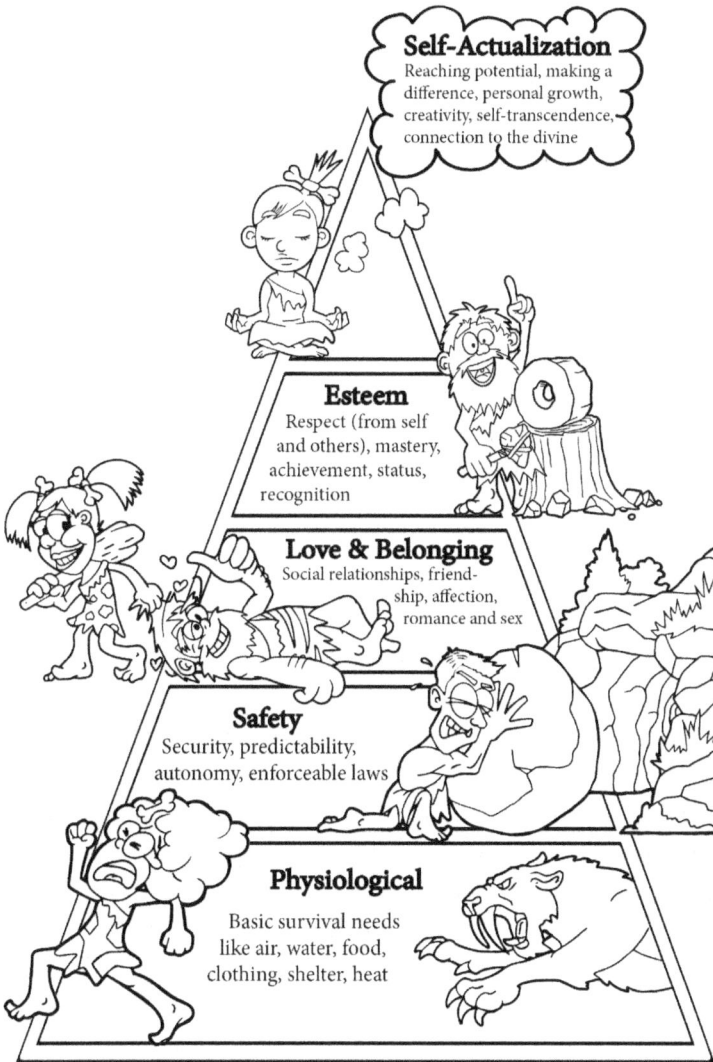

Self-Actualization
Reaching potential, making a difference, personal growth, creativity, self-transcendence, connection to the divine

Esteem
Respect (from self and others), mastery, achievement, status, recognition

Love & Belonging
Social relationships, friendship, affection, romance and sex

Safety
Security, predictability, autonomy, enforceable laws

Physiological
Basic survival needs like air, water, food, clothing, shelter, heat

The premise of Maslow's model is that we have to satisfy our fundamental needs before we meet our higher ones. You're unlikely to write the great American novel if you're dying of starvation. And you probably won't discover a cure for cancer while you're fighting for your life in a war zone.

ADAM

While sex is critical for the species to survive, no individual sexual experience is necessary for personal survival. So why do some people act like they're going to die without porn, if they don't actually need it to survive?

If you were to ask a typical porn user why he does what he does, you might hear:

- I'm bored and it's something to do
- I have a high sex drive
- I'm curious
- I have no idea

The fact is, most guys are clueless that they're using porn to try to fulfill unmet needs. Understanding this becomes a huge eye-opener for them as well as their significant others.

Of course, pornography won't replace air if you're suffocating or food if you're starving to death. On the other end of the spectrum, watching porn won't help anyone accomplish their One True Purpose in life. (And if they think it does, maybe they should be aiming a little higher. Just sayin'.) But those middle tiers of needs: safety, belonging, love, and esteem—porn can trick a person into feeling like those needs are being met for a fleeting moment.

We live in an age of virtual reality. Remember that porn today is more interactive than ever before, with nearly unlimited video content available. People can project themselves into the story and imagine what it would be like to experience having their needs met. Here are some ways porn does this:

SAFETY

Some people have never learned to deal with conflict. Maybe they didn't witness healthy conflict in their family of origin, or they were taught that disagreement is inherently bad. Whatever the reason, any type of confrontation makes them believe their relationship is in danger. And if they don't know how to cope with those feelings, they turn to porn for comfort. While the porn doesn't create a sense of real safety, it can distract them from their fears. Porn becomes like a Band-Aid or a chocolate chip cookie, soothing their painful emotions. Or they may simply use the intense surge of pleasure that porn provides to drown out their unmet needs.

LOVE AND BELONGING

No amount of pornography will ever help someone belong. Usually, the opposite is true—porn disconnects people from each other. But for some guys, watching porn can help them imagine mattering to other people. They can fantasize about being desired when they're actually quite lonely. Multiple studies have found a strong association between loneliness and porn use.[1] When they project themselves into the scenarios they see, people can manufacture a false sense of connection without the messiness and hard work of a real relationship.

That said, simply being around people isn't a cure for loneliness. People can feel even lonelier with others than by themselves if they aren't connecting. To combat loneliness, a person needs to forge meaningful connections with others.

ESTEEM

When a person turns to porn because they have an unmet need for esteem or respect—whether real or imagined—using porn can become a passive-aggressive way to make themselves heard. The thing is, if we're lucky, we grow up in families that teach us how to express emotions verbally. We learn to stand up for ourselves in healthy ways. But if we don't have that skill set, we "act out" our emotions in ways that can be self-destructive, whether it be anger at feeling mistreated, disappointment at not being cared about, etc.

So watching porn can become a person's way to punish others or communicate that they're angry, sad, offended, etc. without risking the consequences of direct confrontation. As dysfunctional as it sounds, it becomes a way of saying, "I will make you miserable if you don't respect me."

As you may have guessed, all these attempts at meeting needs create some problems. First of all, watching porn only provides temporary relief from unmet needs. What's more, porn use feels like a safer way to meet your needs because it lacks all of the risks (such as rejection) associated with real relationships. But the problem is, if you don't have risk and vulnerability in a relationship, you don't have a real relationship.

The good news is, your partner has some clues to help him figure out his unmet needs. If you'll recall from Chapter Eight, emotions are great communicators. If you pay attention to them, certain emotions (especially uncomfortable ones) will alert you of your unmet needs.

RECOGNIZING YOUR EMOTIONS

As a woman, there's a good chance you already have a head start in allowing yourself to both feel and talk about your emotions. In Western society, women are expected to be emotionally self-aware. Even if you happened to be born into a family that didn't really *do* emotion, or if prescribed gender roles aren't your thing, the culture you live in often allows you to be more emotionally expressive than your male counterparts.

What you don't have going for you: women are often told by society to manage their emotions better. Being "too emotional" can be seen as a sign of weakness or an inability to think rationally. A strong and legitimate emotional response from a woman is often dismissed as an "overreaction," which is terribly frustrating. "After all," some people insinuate, "you should be able to logic your way out of how you feel."

WENDY

But men are expected to simply not have emotions at all, although they certainly do. In fact, a 2014 British study[2] on the differences in male and female emotions found just the opposite—not only do men experience emotions, they may be *more intense* for men than for women.

Researchers showed movies to fifteen men and fifteen women while measuring their emotional response through electrodes attached to their skin. The content of the videos was categorized as either blissful, exciting, heartwarming, or funny. After the videos ended, all subjects were questioned about their emotional response, and true to expectations, the women reported a much *higher* emotional response than the men did.

But the electrodes told a different story: based on the data, the men had a higher emotional response than the women in every category. And in the case of heartwarming content, the men reacted twice as strongly as the women, even though they didn't report those intense emotions on the post-study survey. Men may feel more than women do, but they're programmed to express their emotions less.

This study echoed research all the way back in 1974 at the University of Pittsburgh, when sixty-four male and female college students were shown slides designed to evoke various emotions. The women consistently showed greater facial expressions and reported feeling more emotion. But while the men showed less emotion on their faces, once again, the electrodes on the men recorded *more* skin conductance and accelerated heart rate than on the women.

So what's the deal here? The Pitt researchers concluded that women tend to be *externalizers* of emotion, while men are often *internalizers*.[3] Women often appear more *emotive* than men, but that doesn't mean they're more *emotional*.

This all means that you both may have some unlearning to do. Not only does your future husband have to break the basic rules of society to allow himself to express his feelings, he may not even be used to recognizing his feelings as they're happening—or he may be equipped with the Standard Male Emotional Vocabulary™: limited to four terms, "good," "fine," "frustrated," and "mad."

Have you ever tried to start up a conversation with a teenage boy? Unless you're talking to a fairly mature kid, usually the most you can hope to eke out of him is a blank facial expression, no eye contact, and a slew of one-word non-answers to your open-ended questions. Getting a teenage boy to express himself sometimes feels like trying to solve world hunger or get to the front of the line at the DMV in less than ninety minutes.

ADAM

A guy who's developed a porn habit may be a teenager, emotionally speaking—maybe even a preteen. He could have matured in other ways—moved away to college, graduated and found work, learned to support himself and care for others, etc. But if he's been drowning out his painful emotions with the dopamine surges from porn, he probably has very little experience *feeling* his feelings.

Uncomfortable emotions will become an early warning sign for him that a porn relapse could be around the corner. Think about that for a minute. Painful emotion is an early indicator of relapse. Recognizing those emotions will help him to prepare and change course. That's a big deal.

So if either of you have never been taught how to identify and manage difficult emotions, where do you even start?

LEARN TO NAME EMOTIONS AND FEELINGS

WENDY

One life skill that people don't tend to address nearly as much as learning to budget, do your own laundry, or become an accomplished YouTuber is something called *emotional granularity*. [4] Let's say you'd made plans to spend time with someone you care about, but they were called into work at the last minute. And you're upset. But what do you mean when you say you're *upset*? Are you *disappointed*? Do you feel *rejected*? Or *lonely*? Or maybe you're legitimately *angry*. Maybe this happens all the time, and now you're *irate*.

People with high emotional granularity can distinguish between all the different ways of feeling *upset*. It's the ability to know many different terms for emotions and to perceive nuances in your day-to-day feelings. Having high emotional granularity means you can differentiate between *depression* and *anxiety*,[*][5] you can vocalize whether your sister's long list of accomplishments makes you feel *admiration, envy,* or *resentment,* and you can

---

* In a survey of college students, most lumped the two disorders together and couldn't distinguish between their attributes.

describe whether the jitters you feel before performing at a concert are *nervousness* or *excitement*.

Emotional granularity is a life skill that doles out benefits in various areas. People with high emotional granularity go to the doctor less and use less medication. Scientists have even found that the best way to overcome a fear of spiders, of all things, is for arachnophobes to observe and describe how they feel around a spider. In experiments, this soothed their anxiety better than either distracting themselves from the spider or trying to reframe the spider as non-threatening.[6]

So with your partner, you'll want to practice identifying a broad range of emotions. Read more books. Listen to podcasts. Practice asking other people how they're feeling. Try to zero in on their precise emotions. When you watch movies or TV together with your partner, try to identify what each character is feeling in a scene. When your boss snaps at you, try to determine what emotions she was feeling that would have led her to lash out in that way. Find people who are good at describing emotions, and listen to the words they use. Write in a journal about how you feel, and try to label a different emotion each day of the week. In everything you do, look for a variety of emotion words. They will benefit you in all of the ways we described above, *and* they will help your partner uncover the mystery of which unmet needs he is covering up with porn use.

SEARCH YOUR FEELINGS

ADAM

Examining painful emotions is mission critical. This isn't about being a Debbie Downer. Have you ever responded, "I'm fine," when you really weren't? Or "no worries," when your feelings were actually hurt? Or used humor or sarcasm to hide your true feelings? Nobody is on cloud nine all of the time, even though polite society dictates we should at the very least be "fine." But polite society won't help you with a compulsive pornography problem.

As you're expanding your emotional vocabulary, also remember that there are no "bad" or "wrong" emotions—they're simply messengers. Just let them pass through you. And your partner can do the same with his emotions. Think about them. Talk to each other about them. You each have a puzzle to put together. What unmet needs are your emotions signalling? What painful emotions and unmet needs is he suppressing with pornography use?

Now, he might not know at first. That's okay. Take your time. Remember that you're looking for one of those three middle tiers of needs (safety, love/belonging, and esteem/respect). You can ask questions that focus specifically on those core needs:

SAFETY

- Do you feel anxiety or fear about anything coming up?
- Are you afraid of being rejected or abandoned?
- Do any of your relationships feel in danger?

LOVE AND BELONGING

- Do you feel out of place anywhere, like you don't belong?
- Do you feel unloved or unwanted in any of your relationships?
- Have you had any difficult interactions lately with people you are closest to?

ESTEEM

- Do you feel like a failure in any area of your life?
- Have you felt judged by people at work or at school lately?
- Are you afraid you're irrelevant—that you don't matter?

These questions will serve as a springboard for your partner to share more of his emotions and experience as he learns to meet needs he may not have known existed. We also want the same questions to catapult you to a place where you can examine your own needs. And when you're addressing pornography, your own needs will also likely be safety, esteem, love, and belonging.

YOUR OWN NEEDS

By this point in the book, we imagine you've decided that pornography isn't invited to your proverbial dinner table. If that's true, your future husband's commitment to this same ideal will provide some peace for you, even if he's still working toward living it the way he wants.

So if you're like many of the women I've worked with, when you see that your partner isn't taking change seriously or recovery isn't moving as quickly as you'd like, you might worry about the stability and predictability of your future together. Is change really important to him? Does he understand how much this matters to you? Will this ever get better, or are you going to ride this pornified merry-go-round until the end of time?

So you might have some unmet safety, esteem, or love-and-belonging needs of your own. I usually see two ways partners of porn users try to get their needs met in this context: they look for some peace of mind by controlling their partner's behavior, or they ignore the problem and numb out. Maybe you're obsessing about knowing where he is at all times or having complete access to his internet history. Or maybe you're focusing solely on the fun aspects of your relationship: going out, hanging out, making out, hoping if you ignore the problem, it'll go away on its own. Maybe you don't want to ruin your vibe by addressing the hard stuff.

Emotional granularity will help you out here. Stop and take time to listen to your emotions. Try to discover what you're really feeling and why you feel the way you do. If uncomfortable feelings pop up out of nowhere, evaluate which events or thought processes made you feel that way. When you understand your own emotions, you'll be better able to pinpoint your unmet needs and understand the ineffective behaviors you use to try to cope with them.

MEETING BOTH YOUR NEEDS

While there's rarely a direct correlation between a specific unmet need and a specific draw to porn use, discovering his unmet needs will usually be your partner's springboard to self-awareness, which will help him predict relapses long before they happen. So please don't expect a simple formula in which your partner learns to meet his needs and—voilá—his porn use evaporates. Identifying unmet needs is a journey of self-discovery, where greater levels of self-awareness lead to an improved capacity for self-understanding and self-empathy, the effects of which diminish the need for porn use over time.

The following pages identify a couple of ways both of you can be proactive about meeting your needs rather than slipping back into comfortable but dangerous ways of coping. And we'll also show you how you can live peacefully with unmet needs, because not every need can be taken care of with a magic wand.

DIRECTLY ADDRESS NEEDS

When you're examining your unmet needs, you will each begin to identify themes in your life that contribute to your respective coping behaviors. Maybe your boss passes you over for a promotion, which makes you feel unimportant at work. Or some of your friends get together and somehow "forget" to invite you. What if you text a few family members when you're lonely, and no one responds until the next day?

Sometimes all you need to do is address these problems and find workable solutions. Stand up for yourself with your boss, asking for a meeting about her perception of your performance. Maybe you'll find out she does value your contribution and has other plans for you. Confront your friends about leaving you out. You might learn something about them or yourself, or at least know it's time to look for new friends. Determine which family members are reliable, and connect more intentionally with them.

For your partner, meeting these needs may mean the difference between relapsing or sidestepping a trigger to self-medicate with porn. For you, meeting these needs can keep you out of a pattern of emotionally numbing yourself when you feel anxious about your future, or from feeling like you have to control every aspect of your partner's life to prevent a relapse or even have a good day. When solutions are available, seeking to identify and meet needs is a great strategy. Sometimes all you have to do is ask for what you want.

REINTERPRET YOUR NEEDS.

Sometimes my kids whine that they're hungry a whopping five minutes after they ate a huge dinner. Hint: they're not hungry. They're often bored. Or other times I misinterpret my exhaustion at the end of the day as boredom, and I stay up late trying to entertain myself when I really should go to sleep. When our bodies are signaling unmet needs to us, most often through our emotions, we don't always read the signals right the first time. Even when you're certain which need isn't met in your life, you'll often need time to figure out more about it.

As I mentioned earlier, a lot of guys I work with misinterpret their desires to look at porn as a "high sex drive," rather than a way to manage stress, cure boredom, feel valued or loved, or even to assert their independence. As your partner begins to examine his needs, he'll come to know himself better than he ever has.

Reinterpreting your own needs matters too. At first, you may believe your unmet need is a partner who doesn't look at pornography. But look deeper. Why does that matter to you? Look at Maslow's hierarchy again, and see how your concerns fit the middle tiers of needs. Does his porn use make you feel unwanted or unloved? Does the fact that he doesn't immediately stop using porn right after you've discussed it mean he doesn't care about you? Does his porn use endanger the stability of your relationship?

Take time to understand what drives your emotions about his struggle. No matter how badly you want to see measurable changes in him, you have to look for ways to meet your own needs that don't revolve around him. Otherwise, every struggle he has and each step backward he takes, you'll find yourself in more pain than necessary. The two of you may build a life together, but an unhealthy "we" will never compensate for a loss of "I" in the process. We'll give you the specifics about how to accomplish this in Chapter Fourteen.

WENDY

And both of you may also discover whether or not some perceived unmet needs are unfounded. Maybe life is better than you think. Engage with people, such as sponsors, each other, and your support system, to help yourselves see your blind spots. Write about your respective needs. There's something about putting your thoughts out there, especially for other people to experience, that helps you clarify them.

You'll benefit from sharing your thoughts, getting feedback, sleeping on them, and trying again later. Sometimes our fears and perceptions are just that: imagined grievances, unmerited self-loathing, and worst-case scenarios that never materialize.

LETTING GO

Now that you can properly identify your unmet needs, all you have to do is get them met, right? Easy peasy lemon NOPE. I'm sorry to say, it's not that simple. You may be able to formulate a plan to meet certain needs, as we mentioned above. But sometimes you'll both have to be patient while you live with unmet needs.

It would be great if we could identify and meet every single need we ever have. But life is rarely (if ever) ideal like that. Some needs have no easy solution. Or it may take time before they can be met. We all need human companionship, but no one can guarantee when or if they'll get married. Sometimes we have to live with and face our fears, even when we don't feel safe. Some things are simply out of our control, so it's just as important to accept life on its own terms as it is to develop skills for meeting needs.

Think about it: neither of you can *demand* that you'll never feel heartbreak, disappointment, uneasiness, resentment, etc. You can love each other, surround yourselves with people who care about you, choose vocations you excel at, try to afford a home in a safe neighborhood. But your needs often depend on other people and circumstances out of your control. You can't just forget about everyone you're attached to and be sublimely zen. Attachments are scary, but they're part of being human. We live in an unpredictable world, and sometimes life is simply discomfort. That discomfort will mold you both into better people if you allow it to.

In twelve-step meetings, you'll find strength in this part of the serenity prayer: "God, grant me the serenity to accept the things I cannot change, the courage to change the things I can, and the wisdom to know the difference." Instead of turning to porn or trying to control others or avoiding reality in order to cope with discomfort, you can find serenity by letting go of outcomes.

If this sounds easier said than done when the proverbial cow dung hits the fan and sprays all over your life, here are some strategies for letting go:

- Try to imagine worst-case scenarios involving your unmet needs, and realize you can survive even that.
- Think about previous times when life has been difficult but you got through it. Maybe life turned out better than you would have thought, in spite of (or sometimes because of) your misfortune.
- Reframe painful or "negative" outcomes as learning or growing experiences.
- Be gentle with yourself. Treat yourself how you would treat someone you love.
- Practice gratitude for the good stuff. Find ways to appreciate where you're at. Even with some unmet needs, it's seldom all bad. Record these thoughts in a gratitude journal. You'll be amazed at the ways intentional gratitude will shift your perspective on life.
- Practice mindfulness. There are plenty of good books, apps, and other resources that will teach you mindfulness (some of the best ones are listed in Appendix C). Mindfulness is using meditation to become aware of the present moment and accept your feelings, thoughts, body sensations,

and life situation without judgment. It's a skill that takes practice to learn, but plenty of people swear by its ability to help them live peacefully with the distresses of life.

- Trust a higher power's plan for you.

Whatever you or your partner's unmet needs are, be aware that they won't last forever, that you will both have strategies and resources to help you out, and that learning to live with them brings peace, wisdom, and maturity.

GENEVIEVE   APRIL 2013

Genevieve's heavy eyelids lift at the sound of shuffling. The dark shadow of Jacob crawling into bed beside her eclipses the sunlight streaming through the slats in the blinds. He wraps one arm around her waist, then kisses her on the forehead. He rolls back out of bed, grabbing a shirt off of his nightstand and pulling it over his head.

Genevieve shoots straight up, wide awake now.

"Where are you going?"

"Shhhh," Jacob whispers, "Owen's finally asleep. He's been up since four. He didn't want to eat or anything. He's just playing with his rings like a maniac."

"Oh," Genevieve whispers, "Thanks for getting up with him."

"You were dead asleep. It was a long week at the bookstore."

"Yeah. Where are you going? It's Saturday."

"Mark said to be at his house at eight to help load the truck. If I leave now, I'll only be five minutes late."

Genevieve's heart sinks as she covers her face with her hands. "Oh, my gosh. I completely forgot. I think I'm in denial about their move."

"Yeah. It sucks," Jacob whispers as he sits down at the foot of the bed. "They've been great friends."

"Yeah. And I wanted to have some time for just you and me today. I love running our business, but I miss when we could just be friends."

Jacob is silent for a second, then whisper-blurts, "I was keeping it a surprise, but I made reservations for us tonight."

"What? Where? How?"

"I got Brianna down the street to babysit. She's great with the kids."

"Seriously? You're amazing!"

Jacob shushes her again, then says, "At the Oceanaire."

Genevieve's eyes grow big. "You were actually able to get reservations? I can't believe you remembered I wanted to go there!" Her cheeks flush. "I mean, of course you remembered." Then she slumps forward, "We can't afford it, Jacob."

"Actually, I've been putting money away for the past three months to have a night like this. We can afford it. You're worth it."

Genevieve's chest rises, "I'm so excited!"

Jacob ties his shoes.

"And hey, please tell Mark and Jean that I'm going to miss them terribly, especially since they're dead to me for moving away."

Jacob chuckles under his breath. "I will." He kisses her again, on the lips this time. "I'll see you soon. After lunch at the latest."

"Can't wait!" Genevieve calls to Jacob a little too loudly. Down the hall, Owen cries out.

What Genevieve sees ninety minutes later drowns out all the noise of this ordinary Saturday morning. She can't make out the sounds of Maya bossing Owen around in the backyard. She only hears the blood rushing in her ears.

Their internet filter shows a lot of activity. Like, *a lot*. Further back than she can stand to look. When was the last time she checked the filter? The vile names of some of the sites drain the color from her face. Is this a disgusting joke? Were they hacked? She doesn't feel alone in her house anymore. She feels creepy eyes staring at her, but from where? Are her kids safe in her own backyard? She reaches for her phone. Jacob will know what to do. *Jacob.*

No, Jacob had those kinds of problems before. Long ago, when they were single. Well, there was that one time just after they were married... But they worked that out. Plus, he would tell her. She'd always liked how honest Jacob was.

And they had a great marriage. A really great marriage. They fought a lot. But that's what people who love each other do. Running the store together is stressful. Jacob wouldn't do *that*. He loved her, right? He'd sacrificed his whole engineering career for her. He'd followed her to small-town Minnesota to run a bookstore with her.

Right?

Genevieve composes a text, fingers flying.

But what if...?

No.

What was more likely, some hacker invading their network to look at porn, or her husband who lived here?

He's had problems before.

Just when Genevieve doesn't think the pit in her stomach could get any deeper, the bottom falls out.

JACOB

Jacob's lugging half of a couch when his phone buzzes.

"I think you got a text, man," Mark mumbles from the other side of the couch.

"Yeah. Let's just put this on its side at the back." Jacob tries to conceal his panting breath as he walks backward up the ramp into the moving truck. They're only getting started, and Jacob seems more out of shape than he realized. But he wanted to support the only friends he and Genevieve have made in Minnesota.

Jacob pulls his phone from his pocket and opens the text from Genevieve.

I just found A LOT of pornography on our internet filter. You'd better come home and explain this to me RIGHT NOW.

He reads it twice.

Jacob looks out of the truck. Jean laughs about something with her sister, holding a box on the lawn. Just a normal day.

He looks back at his phone and reads the text again, trying to think. *Now. It's happening now.*

Maybe he can explain himself, maybe there's a way to tell Genevieve that won't blow up their marriage...

No. This is it. All the waiting, all the lying, all the looking over his shoulder, and it's finally here. He always imagined he would fix it, that someday he would tell Genevieve everything when it was an old story from a different life. But he was never going to fix it. Each tale he told Genevieve, and the ones he told himself, only seemed to entangle him more.

"You okay, dude?"

Jacob looks up from his phone at Mark. "Yeah, I, uhhh..."

What should he do? It's ruined now. He looks over at Jean and her sister again, walking toward the truck, moving in slow motion. He'll be a jerk to just ditch Mark and Jean on moving day. No one will even know why he left. But he can't make Genevieve wait.

She'll be furious. And devastated.

He has to go home. No more stories. This is it.

Jacob swallows, feeling the pulse in his forehead. "Mark, I have to go." He looks around at the stacked boxes, thinks of the furniture in every room of the house, hours of work left to do. "I'm sorry, man."

"Oh." Mark scratches his cheek. "Yeah, that's okay, Jake. You don't have to be sorry."

Man, you have no idea.

1   Yoder, Vincent Cyrus, Thomas B. Virden III, and Kiran Amin. "Internet Pornography and Loneliness: An Association?." *Sexual Addiction & Compulsivity* 12, no. 1 (2005): 19-44.

Butler, Mark H., Samuel A. Pereyra, Thomas W. Draper, Nathan D. Leonhardt, and Kevin B. Skinner. "Pornography Use and Loneliness: A Bidirectional Recursive Model and Pilot Investigation." *Journal of Sex & Marital Therapy* 44, no. 2 (2018): 127-137.

2   Withnall, Adam. "Father's Day 2014: Study Shows Men Are More Emotionally Sensitive." *The Independent*, June, 2014. Accessed June, 2020. https://www.independent.co.uk/news/uk/home-news/father-s-day-2014-study-shows-men-are-more-emotionally-sensitive-than-women-they-re-just-also-better-9532945.html (accessed June 19, 2017).

3   Buck, Ross, Robert E. Miller, and William F. Caul. "Sex, Personality, and Physiological Variables in the Communication of Affect via Facial Expression." *Journal of Personality and Social Psychology* 30, no. 4 (1974): 587.

4   Barrett, Lisa Feldman. *How Emotions Are Made: The Secret Life of the Brain.* New York: Mariner Books, 2017.

5   Barrett, Lisa Feldman. *How Emotions Are Made: The Secret Life of the Brain.* New York: Mariner Books, 2017.

6   Barrett, Lisa Feldman. *How Emotions Are Made: The Secret Life of the Brain.* New York: Mariner Books, 2017.

12. STONE #3:
CHOOSING ACCOUNTABILITY

Act as if what you do makes a difference. It does.
—William James

WENDY

Without relationships, we'd never grow. If we each had our own desert island to ourselves, how would we come to know our own faults? How would we learn sacrifice and selflessness?

In Antoine de St. Exupéry's timeless novel, *The Little Prince*, the title character lives all alone on a tiny asteroid about the size of a house. He's lonely but otherwise content. He has zero responsibility and no one to worry about. But when a rose grows on the planet, he falls in love with her. And everything changes. Both the prince and the rose are selfish at first—neither know how to truly care for one another and put the other's needs before their own. It's only when the prince leaves the planet, meets people, and befriends a wise fox on Earth that he starts to grow up. Through others, he learns what it means to be responsible for the people he loves.

I was a bit like the little prince before I was married. I mean, I knew people, and I had plenty of friends, but I'd never shared a life so closely with someone the way married people do. I guess I thought I'd make a fine spouse. No sweat, right?

But my first year of marriage was a bit of a shock. I came from a family with an unspoken rule that we did not talk about our feelings—not the bad ones, at least. I guess the thinking was that if we only focused on happy things, we'd always be happy. But I married a man who wanted to hear about all of my emotions, and not expressing them meant to him that I wasn't making an effort to connect. I know—total gender-role reversal. It might not sound like a big deal, but in the little microcosm of our marriage, it was. Most of our fights the first year of our marriage went something like this:

> Peter: You never talk about your feelings!
> Me: I don't want to talk about my feelings!
> Peter: Okay. But can we at least discuss how you feel about that?
> END SCENE

So it took me a while, but I eventually got over being offended that my spouse wanted me to change something about myself. I learned to discuss my emotions because it was important to Peter. And now he can't get me to shut up about my feelings. I'm a healthier person for it. That kind of commitment to make changes in ourselves for the people we love is the driving force behind accountability.

ADAM

Accountability is pretty simple in theory. It's taking responsibility for how our actions and choices affect other people, and it's a major element of all healthy relationships. Businesses routinely institute accountability among employees to maximize productivity. And citizens are rightfully outraged when their governments aren't transparent about what's happening behind closed doors. And it just so happens that accountability is going to be one of the most vital tools in your battle with pornography.

Personal accountability comes from a place of empathy. Accountable people are willing to go a mile in the beat-up shoes of the people they love. They're the type of people who help others load up a moving van, even if there are a million things they'd rather do, because they know they'd want the help themselves.

Accountability is also rooted in humility, in the awareness that the sun doesn't rise and set for you alone, in the knowledge that you're not perfect and your actions can hurt others. It's taking responsibility for your part without blaming anyone else. Humble people can even believe they're right about something and *still* take responsibility because of the impact their actions have on others. Empathy is choosing to do something on behalf of another person, and humility is not bragging about it.

When I was first married, I was doing some laundry and had a load of towels I was folding on our uncomfortable futon. My wife looked over and asked, "Can I show you how to fold towels?" Of course, being the independent twenty-six-year-old that I was, I retorted with something like, "I've been folding towels for a decade. I'm good." She said, "No, really. There's a better way to do it." This reminds me of young, optimistic couples who haven't had their first fight and wonder what in the world they could possibly argue about after they get married. What could married people possibly fight about? Answer: everything, including how to fold towels.

The towel-folding saga went on for the next seven *years*. Lindsay respected my autonomy to fold towels man-style, but was relentless in her desire to open my eyes to the brave new world of proper towel folding. One day during that fateful eighth year of marriage, I was folding towels and watching TV. My wife started folding some towels next to me. I had my stack, and she had hers. She then followed me to the linen closet. I crammed my awkward stack of "folded" towels between two shelves and gave the pile a shove for good measure.

My wife took an equal number of carefully folded towels and gently placed them next to my towel-splosion in the closet. I stood there uncomfortably for a moment. Apparently, there is a law of physics, which I clearly don't understand, that allows the same mass of towels to take up less volume if folded in a magical way. The lesson was obvious: I should listen to my wife more. This was actually a turning point in my marriage, when I started to figure out that I wasn't always right. It's embarrassing to admit now, but I've had to learn some of life's simplest lessons the hard way.

I had stubbornly refused to accept that her approach to folding wasn't just a preference but an actual improvement in space management. The take-home message here is this: just because the way I do something *technically* works, it doesn't mean there isn't a better way. Humbly implementing feedback from others can have enormous benefits.

Back in Chapter Nine, we talked about how novelty seeking seems to be hardwired into human programming. And while novelty seeking has likely given humans certain evolutionary advantages over the course of our existence, when left unchecked, obsessing over the next new and interesting thing can keep us from living a connected, fulfilling life. If you'll recall, self-transcendence, along with persistence, is necessary for keeping novelty seeking from going from a useful survival skill to a pointless exercise in excess. As building blocks of accountability, empathy and humility happen to be foundational to self-transcendence, the awareness that you are only one small part of the massive expanse of existence, and only one person with needs among many.

HOW TO PRACTICE ACCOUNTABILITY

The best type of accountability is proactive. Reactive accountability, the kind that only kicks in once you've made a major misstep, is immature. Reactive accountability is admitting you had your hand in the cookie jar only after the nanny cam ratted you out, when you tell the truth because you were caught. You'll never stop hurting people if you only ever take accountability after you've hurt them. You'll always be playing relational catch-up.

Proactive accountability involves anticipating problems and cutting them off at the pass. There are several ways to accomplish this:

- Stop yourself the moment you realize you've hurt

someone and ask for a do-over
- Acknowledge how you've injured someone before they bring it to your attention
- Make a plan about how to avoid causing harm in the future
- Identify behaviors that put you at risk for hurting others, and eliminate them from your life

By far, one of the best tools your partner can use to break a porn habit is to practice proactive accountability with you and others. It's easier to pull a weed when it's an inch tall, not when it's grown into a thorny monstrosity with birds nesting in it. And brushing your teeth is always more pleasant than a root canal. The type of accountability we're about to show you will give your future husband superhuman foresight into possible relapses long before his brain can be hijacked by porn's magical powers.

WENDY

Practicing accountability is personal, and it's an evolving process. You may choose to practice it differently than another couple would. Best-selling author and blogger Gretchen Rubin has discovered that we all respond to expectations differently.[1] Some people need accountability to get anything done. They don't achieve goals unless they feel outside pressure to accomplish them, whether that be in the form of an accountability partner, an authority figure, or a mentor whom they need to report to.

Others do well setting and achieving goals independently, and the idea of reporting progress to another person feels like uncomfortable and unnecessary pressure. And yet other people aren't great at achieving goals regardless of internal or external expectations. For them, they achieve the most when they feel like they truly *want* to accomplish something, regardless of goals or expectations. Rubin's book is a great place to start if you want to understand how you and your partner each respond to expectations.

ADAM

But no matter your partner's accountability style, if he finds that he's not making progress in recovery, increasing accountability is a great place to start. My clients who practice accountability experience major reductions in pornography use compared to those who don't.

Having accountability conversations together may help you to feel included in and updated on his recovery, so you don't have to guess how he's doing. As a couple, you'll need to figure out what works for you. That said, in the absence of professional support or guidance, starting out with a consistent, daily five-minute accountability conversation is your best bet. Ideally, he'll be the one to initiate these conversations with you. We'll give you some tips later in this chapter about how to have these conversations.

Over time, maybe you'll both find the formality of accountability conversations a little stiff and prefer to keep communication lines open in more organic ways. If you start to feel like you're his mother keeping tabs on him, it's fine to pull back and renegotiate how you'll have these conversations. Or these discussions may make you both feel more connected. Either way, it's important to note that as his partner, you have a right to know anything about his thoughts, feelings, and behavior that are material to the health and safety of your relationship.

You'll also get to decide how much detail you're comfortable hearing—if you want to know all about every trigger he experiences, or it's more productive for you to only hear about the Big Stuff. Some women find comfort in hearing all the details. If they know exactly what their husband is experiencing, knowing it's not worse than they imagined brings them some peace. But plenty of women become distressed by knowing all of the fine print about every trigger and slip. You shouldn't have to bear that weight if you don't want to.

In fact, some people working recovery use reporting slips as a crutch to hand off their responsibility for their actions to another person. Accountability should be a way for him to work through his patterns and behavior through an accountability partner's feedback, not to transfer his responsibility for his actions to that individual.

Whatever you decide about accountability between the two of you, you can't be the only person he's accountable to. He doesn't want to lose you, and he's probably on his best behavior around you. If you were his sole accountability partner, there's a chance he'd spin his reporting in a way that protects you from emotional pain and shields himself from irreversible consequences—particularly if fear and shame are his primary motivators. And depending on your relationship, you may find it difficult to hear the level of detail he needs to give to be truly accountable and find workable solutions.

(Side note: his mom can't be his accountability partner either, for the same reasons. He'll need another guy in his life to be accountable to.)

Many compulsive porn users choose to be accountable to a sponsor, often from a twelve-step program. If no sponsor is available, he can choose someone he trusts from his group of helpers we discussed in Chapter Ten.

WENDY

I met a vibrant woman named Mariana at a coffee shop one weekday morning. She was able to schedule forty-five minutes to talk to me between dropping kids at school, picking up a few groceries, and heading to her job at the local university where she teaches and works as a therapist. She told me all about her life before the one she has now, when she was a college student, falling head over heels for a guy named Danny.

They'd been dating for four months. They were hanging out on a bean bag chair one night, just enjoying one another's company, when Danny blurted out in one breath, "I have something to tell you. I've been addicted to pornography since I was ten."

Mariana was surprised, but not repulsed. She thought of herself as an open and understanding person, and she wanted to be accepting. From Danny's perspective, he'd just disclosed something significant. He was serious about Mariana, and she was the first girl he'd ever told about his porn use. But Mariana didn't really know what to do with the information. She didn't yet know what this type of compulsion entailed.

"I didn't know about the moods, the coping," she told me.

Over the next eight months of dating, Danny would occasionally mention times when he was struggling. But Mariana didn't know how to ask what that meant. She didn't know she was allowed to ask private details about his struggle. She thought love and acceptance were all Danny needed.

But everything changed once they were married. Danny's relapses started to affect Mariana in a devastating way. Her compassion dissolved into blinding anger, which surprised her. Danny's issues no longer seemed to be about a high sex drive that just needed to be satiated by loving intimacy. Now Danny's relapses looked like cheating, like betrayal. Plus, Danny's drive to lie was a lot stronger now.

"When we were dating, he would be so honest with me. I could see the difference between the addict and the man he really was. I've always loved how honest he is when he's truly himself," she told me.

They were sexually active now, and Mariana needed reassurances that she was wanted. " I was thinking, 'We're having sex now! This is not okay! Am I not good enough?'" She began comparing herself to the women Danny was watching, and it was messing with her head. Danny lied more to keep from upsetting Mariana.

In her turn, Mariana tried to take ownership of it all and police him. Danny was an IT professional and spent all of his days with computers. She found herself triggered by the smallest details, like when Danny would tell her he'd had a hard day. "My mind would start racing. 'When is he gonna relapse again?'" she told me. She was hurt and exhausted.

They went on this way for another four years, while Mariana finished her master's degree and bore a son. Danny secretly relapsed every four months, almost like clockwork, but Mariana could tell anyway by his selfish, moody behavior.

When I contacted Mariana eighteen months after our first coffee-shop date to catch up on her story before publication, her husband Danny was eager to meet with me too to tell his story. When I met with both of them over Zoom, I could see why they're a couple. Mariana's vibrance and warmth compliment Danny's stoic intellectualism. It was interesting to hear the same story from his perspective.

Danny took me back to the beginning of his compulsions, before puberty even set in. He was a bullied kid with self-esteem issues, and even though the internet hadn't yet become a household item, he found escape and acceptance in soap opera sex scenes and underwear ads in the mail. At fourteen, once the internet became a thing, Danny was sucked into a world where he could feel good about himself and leave the awkward, pimply kid behind while he watched porn. This otherwise straight-laced kid once broke into his educator mother's office at school one night to watch pornography. He got caught and lied about it.

The beginning of his story is one you've heard again and again throughout this book. He confessed his addiction to his pastor in college, who meant well but gave him unhelpful advice. Later in college, he confessed to another pastor, who sent him to an on-campus cognitive-behavioral therapy group. While this helped Danny understand his porn use a bit, the techniques didn't improve his behaviors. More of the same happened with a few ensuing therapists. "I wasn't yet in a place where the pain of the solution was less than the pain of acting out," he told me.

After a failed relationship in which Danny broke it off with a girl he was serious about marrying when he realized the only thing they had in common was physical attraction, Danny met Mariana. They were drawn to each other's intelligence and got lost in hours of conversation late into the night over shakes at Ben and Jerry's. And the rest is history.

Except history often isn't simple. History usually involves some dark days and battles fought. "At that point, partially due to my addiction, I had no understanding of a relationship with the opposite sex. I was physically acting out my addiction with Mariana."

Once they were married, Danny became aware of the pain he was causing Mariana. He would wait days to tell her about a relapse, often after they'd already been intimate, which upset her more.

When they started talking about having kids and trying to conceive, Danny tried everything, from attending a support group at his church for compulsive porn users to meeting with his pastor to writing out a "report card" to give Mariana each night before bed, in which he'd grade himself in various areas of healthy living, but it all only seemed to add to Mariana's stress.

"I was still trying to do it on my own terms," Danny told me. He was lost. All he wanted was to stop breaking his wife's heart. But nothing would really change until their first son was eighteen months old.

Deliverance arrived on an ordinary Sunday morning during a weekly men's meeting at church. A man who was permanently confined to a wheelchair rolled up to the front of the room and started to share about his recovery from pornography use.

"I would never—" Danny told me. "You couldn't pay me enough money, you couldn't threaten me enough, with people from the neighborhood in a spiritual setting, for me to talk about something so personal, so vulnerable. But he did! At that point, I wanted to understand him more."

That afternoon, Danny gave him a call. The man, Leonard, asked if Danny had a sponsor. None of the groups Danny had attended did sponsors. Danny told Leonard his story.

"Well, you've certainly tried a lot. You've been around the block. Now do you want to try what works?" Leonard asked.

"Yeah, that's why I'm calling you," Danny said.

Leonard became Danny's sponsor. He told Danny to go to weekly Sexaholics Anonymous meetings and work the twelve steps. That was in 2012. It wasn't smooth sailing from there. Danny still relapsed sometimes. But according to Mariana, he started to be honest about his relapses. And he stopped blaming his wife and other circumstances for his relapses. He began to take responsibility. He also started working through difficult emotions when they arose, without relapsing every time. Things were changing.

Danny counts May 25, 2013 as his sobriety date. He's been

sober for seven and a half years now. And Mariana has recovered from her trauma as well. You can see it in her eyes, in the confidence in her voice. "At the end of the day, you need to be okay with his choices, I've learned." Despite all her attempts to control the situation, Mariana eventually realized she couldn't will him to get help. He had to make that choice on his own.

"Of course, you can choose to be supportive," she admits. "But you can't change any outcomes. And hearing all the details can create anxiety—or it did for me. So I'm glad that he has a sponsor to tell the details to. He needs to be honest about relapses and be able to reassure his wife that he's been 100% honest with his sponsor. That's the conversation we have when he's slipped or relapsed— were you 100% honest with your sponsor? A sponsor can only help if you've been 100% honest."

But of course, Mariana always gets to decide how much information she can tolerate. It's not Danny's choice to protect her from information. That means Mariana needs to tune into her emotions and ask herself if her desire to hear details is anxiety-driven. She needs to think about why she has to know what she does and set appropriate boundaries.

Having that sponsor who understands has made all the difference for Danny. And Mariana gets it. "Because, you don't *know* how he feels, but a sponsor does. With a sponsor, a porn user can see 'he [recovered], and I can do it too.' The fact is, I can try to empathize, but I don't know viscerally how he feels. But with a sponsor, he can realize, 'I don't have to hide anything from you, because I *am* you.'"

"I still go to the same group, still have the same sponsor," Danny tells me. Then he sits quietly for a second looking down at his lap before he looks back at me and starts to speak again:

"I'm not gonna say that it's not been a bumpy ride, because it certainly has been. Working the steps has not been easy, as I've had to come to terms with my defects. I'm not ever going to be a 'normal' person, and I can't do 'normal' things. I can't live my life in a way other people do. I can't have access to things that other people have access to. And that's okay. Because recovery and sobriety are a heck of a lot more important to me than being able to flip open Netflix and watch whatever I want. For the past six years, I've gotten up at 5:30 to meditate and exercise. That's how I start my day, and that's part of my recovery.

"My story is one of willingness. I started with a small amount of willingness, and that willingness grew over time until I now understand that I could relapse tomorrow. I could relapse tonight. I am powerless over my addiction. I'm powerless over my obsessive nature to control other people. There are so many things in my life that I'm powerless over, and it's so much easier to surrender them to a power greater than myself and have him dictate what I should do instead. I've become grateful for this part of myself because it's taught me what humility and surrender really mean. The singular decision to call that man and his willingness to work with me saved my life."

YOUR ACCOUNTABILITY CONVERSATIONS

ADAM

From thousands of hours of therapy with hundreds of clients, I've found that the best accountability conversations should be about highlighting unmet needs, discussing emotions, and identifying risk factors for relapse. Each accountability conversation will look different.

These conversations can be structured or unstructured, depending on your needs. But if you find these conversations aren't working for you, you may need to adjust them one way or another. Also, these discussions should review the past and look toward the future—analyzing both what you could have done differently *and* anticipating how to deal with upcoming issues.

If your partner initiates these conversations, it'll go a long way in establishing trust. But let's say he struggles to instigate these discussions. Again, you don't want to become an interrogator or try to control the situation. But it's important to let him know that if you don't have accountability conversations, the relationship will stagnate, and you won't be able to move forward.

Here are the most helpful items to share:

TRIGGERS

Relapses don't just happen. There is always a trail of triggers and emotions (that often go ignored) leading to every relapse. A trigger is a stimulus—something you see, hear, feel, experience, or remember—that puts you in danger of relapse. Triggers can be sexual in nature. They may include sexual images from the past that pop into his head. He may also run into sexual triggers in everyday life, which amps up his sexual energy. We live in a pretty sexualized world, so seeing sexual imagery in the world around you is really common.

He may also experience emotional triggers—painful or uncomfortable emotions that he wants to avoid or simply doesn't know how to handle—emotions that he's used porn to cope with in the past.

Being accountable about triggers reduces their influence, much like naming an emotion can keep it from overwhelming you, but also because it takes away the secrecy. Secrecy leads to shame, and in order to overcome porn as a coping mechanism, he needs to overcome shame.

When he's sharing triggers, he could say some version of the following:

- Some memories of porn I've watched have entered my mind today.
- Something I saw on TV today felt sexually triggering to me.
- I've been feeling really lonely lately, and that's often an emotional trigger that leads me to want to look at porn to cope.

BOTTOM LINES AND SLIPS

In a nutshell, a *bottom line* is any boundary that your partner has committed to not cross again. Porn use will be a bottom line for him. But on further examination, he'll discover other things he does, behaviors that may seem innocuous but often precede porn use.

187

How does his porn use start? What's his ritual? Does he first scroll aimlessly through social media? Does he stay up late at night after everyone has gone to bed? Does he start with news sites, rationalizing that he's just staying informed about life, but then usually ends up slipping into porn use? Instead of focusing all of his energy on avoiding porn, setting up some boundaries around risky behaviors can make a huge difference. Whatever path he takes to porn, he needs to become aware of the precursors to porn use, even the ones that may seem harmless, and adjust his life accordingly.

Hebb's axiom dictates that "neurons that fire together, wire together." In the same way that Pavlov's dogs started to salivate at the sound of a bell because their brains now connected that bell to food, if he watches porn when he's sad, pretty soon his brain will remind him about porn whenever he's feeling down. For best results, he can set bottom lines around the precursors.

For example, if he often relapses back into porn use when he's feeling resentful about how he's treated, he obviously can't decide he'll never feel resentful again. Remember, emotions can have a mind of their own. But what he can set a bottom line around is how he normally responds to resentment. If he usually shuts down-- which eventually leads to relapse because he uses porn to cope with overwhelming emotions--then the bottom line is "no more shutting down." The boundary he sets for himself is that instead of shutting down he will open up, share his feelings, offload the pain, and get help. That's a bottom line.

How will he know which behaviors require bottom lines and which are normal and safe? If you two are working on this together, you'll likely need to engage in a little trial and error. For some guys, playing video games is a fun distraction. For others, obsessively gaming and avoiding real life often predicts a round of porn use. For some guys, quiet alone time is energizing and healthy. Other guys haven't yet learned to cope with the quiet and turn to porn any time there's no one else around. Some guys can get by with sharing only the most powerful negative emotions and still keep themselves healthy. For other guys, even the slightest amount of sadness or anger can spiral into a porn relapse.

So he has to come to know himself. He can study his own patterns, his feelings, his thoughts, and learn where he needs bottom lines and boundaries in his life as he's gaining skills to deal with how pornography has become a primary form of coping or avoidance.

EMOTIONS AND UNMET NEEDS

Accountability conversations aren't just about making one another aware of dangerous territory for sexual slips. These conversations should be about holistic well-being. As we discussed in the last chapter, your partner's awareness of his emotions and needs, as well as his ability to discuss them openly with you, will help him to both anticipate porn use and become a healthier human in general.

Some examples of what either of you might share:

- I'm feeling really lonely right now, which is a trigger for me. Can we talk?
- I just noticed that I'm really mad and resentful right now. I'm worried this will put me in danger.
- I really need to open up about how I'm feeling.
- I think I just need a break from life stress right now. I'm not giving myself any time to have fun. Can you help me figure out how to manage that?

SELF-CARE

So many of the guys I work with in counseling essentially use pornography as one of their primary forms of self-care. Or rather, they seek out porn instead of turning to true self-care. It's how they pass the time when they're bored. It's how they entertain themselves. It's how they avoid uncomfortable emotions. As we discussed in the last chapter, it's how they cope with unmet needs. Self-care is a need people often don't understand or utilize in the way they should.

Self-care isn't just having fun, relaxing, or engaging in activities to make yourself feel good. Self-care is taking action to ensure you're living a healthy, successful life. During accountability conversations, he can talk about what he's doing to keep himself emotionally balanced. He can talk about completing important tasks he's been avoiding. He can mention how he's made time to enjoy a hobby and remember that life can be rich and fulfilling. He can discuss how he's been taking care of himself physically by getting more rest, by taking a hike in nature, by finding an outlet for his excess energy, by playing basketball with friends. He can tell how he had a difficult conversation with someone that led to reconciliation. He can describe how he's engaging in spiritual or religious rituals that help him feel more purpose or meaning in life.

When I say spirituality, I'm not necessarily talking about religion. For some people, religion and spirituality are intertwined. For others, they're not. When I say spirituality, I mean intentional choices to feel connected or bonded to God, humanity, other people that you care about, your purpose in life, etc. Spirituality is a sense that your life has meaning, that you are more than a pile of molecules spinning around in space, here to consume oxygen for a moment, then obliterated. Spirituality is the sense that your life can be beautiful and transcendent—that your influence on others can leave behind indelible ripples when you are gone.

And as with successes, I find that guys who practice intentional spirituality tend to fare better when trying to kick a porn habit than guys who don't, because spirituality gives their behaviors and choices a much larger context. They start to think and care about the person they want to become.

When he's being accountable about self-care, your partner could share something like:

- Yesterday, I finally finished the school project I've been avoiding for months.
- This morning, I went for a jog. I've been missing exercise with how busy I've been.
- I'm planning on taking the second half of my workday off tomorrow to go to the doctor and see if some medication would help my depression.

YOUR OWN SPONSOR

WENDY

You'll also have the option to choose a sponsor for yourself. Having a sponsor of your own who understands what you've been through can be invaluable. We met Edwin in Chapter Five when his fiancée ghosted him, and we met his new girlfriend Penny in Chapter Six. When Edwin started to take recovery seriously, Penny got a sponsor of her own, a woman who'd once been in deep trauma over her husband's pornography use but had found serenity. Even though Penny had never experienced trauma in the same way many married women do, she found a lot of value in her sponsor. She could turn to her sponsor to know what to expect in her relationship, to talk through her anxieties, and to know she wasn't alone.

Almost all of the women I interviewed had sponsors who provided a listening ear and constructive feedback. Sponsorship offers hope by connecting you to someone who's made it farther down the road than you are. She'll show you what's worked for her and give you options to navigate your partner's porn use and recovery.

Your sponsor can also hold you accountable when you're catastrophizing or crossing into unhealthy coping, like unmanaged rage and anger, emotional numbing, or control. She can help you see when you're micromanaging your partner's recovery or other aspects of your life to cope (e.g., trying to control your body with an eating disorder). Or if you're numbing out, locking yourself in your room eating ice cream and wallowing to the soundtrack of Taylor Swift's "Evermore" for three days. Or if you're blinded by rage and getting into vicious arguments. A sponsor can be a sounding board to help you live a healthier life.

Sponsorship and accountability conversations can also help you stay motivated through the long middle of recovery, when it's hard to see the forest for the trees. In the next chapter, we'll delve into a few other tools to help keep your motivation high.

GENEVIEVE   APRIL 2013

Maya took the Etch-a-Sketch.

Owen screams, "MOM-EE!"

"Hey, he had it for like five hours!"

Genevieve looks limply at the chaos, but she can't muster the words to referee it right now. Less than three hours ago, she and Jacob were planning the night of a lifetime at The Oceanaire. Now the sunlight through the windows, the chirping of birds, the sounds of passing cars all seem strange to her.

How did this happen? What does he even get from it?

She'd stumbled on her dad watching porn once. He'd slammed the computer shut and looked at the ground like she wasn't there. At one point, each of her then-teenage brothers had tattled to Genevieve that he had caught the other one watching porn. Maybe it was a guy thing. But the internet history spanned months, maybe more. How could he lie to her face this whole time and act like nothing was wrong?

Why did she let herself trust him? She closes her eyes, feeling the familiar heat in her chest. She should have been looking for clues all along. She should have known better.

All those years. Everything they shared. Did she even really know Jacob?

The front door creaks open. Without thinking, Genevieve turns away from the footsteps, deafening above Owen's wailing.

"Genevieve..."

"DAD-EE!" Owen screams.

"KIDS. Go outside. Both of you," she snaps, without meaning to.

"But Mommy, we just came back in." Maya frowns.

"Kids, you heard your mom. Go play outside."

Jacob's voice lacks force, but Maya sets down the Etch-a-Sketch and makes her way toward the back door. Owen follows right behind.

Genevieve makes herself look at Jacob.

He's all white and hunched. Like a deflated ghost. "Genevieve. I should have told you. I'm so, so sorry."

He doesn't sit down.

"No! No sorries! I don't want any more stories," Genevieve says through clenched teeth.

Jacob looks at the floor and shifts uncomfortably.

Genevieve closes her eyes to still the beast inside, but tears pour through. "How long?"

"What?"

"How long have you been watching porn behind my back?"

Jacob pauses, then quietly says, "Four years."

Genevieve lets out a strange sound, maybe a choked cry. Possibly a growl.

Their entire marriage. Their entire marriage was a lie.

"Where? How?"

Jacob takes a deep breath, looking at his toes. "Uhh, well... Late at night. When you were at the bookstore. When I was at the bookstore. In the back. Wherever."

Genevieve wants to scream, but the steadiness of her voice surprises her. "I can't do this."

"Wait... what do you mean?"

"I can't *be* in a relationship with someone who's... who's *cheating* on me." Genevieve steels herself for his accusation that she's too emotional, that she's overreacting. But it doesn't come.

"You'll... You'll just leave me?" Jacob swallows.

The thought of a life without Jacob stops her breath.

But let him think that. He *should* think she would leave.

"How would you feel if I just went off and had an affair with some guy and hid it from you?"

Jacob opens his mouth, but seconds pass before he responds, "I would be devastated."

They wait in strained silence. For minutes. Maybe hours.

It's Jacob who breaks the steely air between them, startling Genevieve as he sits down next to her. "We should go to counseling. I went years ago, and it helped. Well, the porn didn't stop. But I was getting there. Together, we could beat this."

Her eyes meet Jacob's, just for a second. He has his wide-eyed questioning look, the one he had the day Genevieve came back to his apartment. After he gave her the letter that was supposed to end it all.

She should slap him, but the tiniest part of Genevieve wants to reach out for his hand, make it all better. She looks past Jacob through the sliding glass door at the kids in the yard. They're crouched on the ground together, examining something small. A bug. Or maybe a worm. Maya seems to be explaining something to Owen, who laughs.

She looks back at Jacob. Nothing makes sense. She doesn't grab his hand. "Okay. Whatever. Find a counselor."

Jacob exhales. "I'm so, so, so sorry, Genevieve. But we'll fix this. *I* will fix this."

Maybe. Maybe someday she won't feel like hiding under her blankets and never coming out. But this has happened before, and a gnawing sense that nothing will ever change just won't leave.

1 Rubin, Gretchen. *The Four Tendencies: The Indispensable Personality Profiles That Reveal How to Make Your Life Better (and Other People's Lives Better Too)*. New York: Harmony Books, 2017.

13. STONE #4: UNDERSTANDING MOTIVATION

To be human is to strive for transcendence.
  —Reza Aslan

WENDY

I have a neighbor, a quiet but friendly gentleman named Bill. A sixty-five-year-old grandfather, Bill is retired now. He's also an ultramarathon runner. He's completed races over fifty miles long without stopping for more than a bathroom break or a quick bite to eat. Just last year, he raced a 26.2-mile marathon in each state.

For those of you who are counting, that's one marathon per week, with a couple of weeks off for the holidays. He once tripped and cracked his head open during a race and ended up stuck in the medic's tent, frustrated and itching to run. They only let him out after he signed a series of forms promising neither he nor his family would sue the race's organizers if he died along the trail. He finished that race too.

Bill is a particularly inspiring example, but he's not alone in his love for running. Over five hundred and seventy marathons are held each year in the United States alone. What on earth is driving people to run crazy distances without any tangible reward when they could be chillin' at home, sleeping or staring at their phones? What's their motivation?

One night at a neighborhood party, I asked Bill why he started running marathons later in life. I think I was secretly hoping for some sort of inspiring sound byte for this book, something like, "I wanted to be the old guy who proved everyone wrong," or "accomplishing great things makes me feel alive." Or even, "Old age be damned, I love the feel of the wind in my hair, the cool sweat on my brow, and the fire burning in my lungs." You know what he told me? "My daughters were getting into running, so I thought I'd give it a try too."

While his response was a letdown for Adam (I, for one, found it funny and interesting), in a way, his accomplishments spoke for themselves. I suspect the reason Bill gave me such a nonchalant answer was because the other answers seemed to go without saying. Of course people do amazing things just to do amazing things. The whole idea of the indomitable human spirit is somehow built into our DNA. He doesn't have to articulate it to tell us that.

For years, scholars and behavioral scientists didn't necessarily believe that. They theorized that the lone driver behind motivation, the reason we make every single choice we do, is simply to seek out pleasure and avoid pain. Sounds a little cynical but fairly intuitive, right? It isn't true, though. In recent years, motivation researchers have discovered that humans are a lot more complex than that. In certain situations, we're willing to sacrifice a pleasurable outcome or walk straight into pain in order to achieve something bigger.[1]

This fascinating characteristic about human nature is the other piece of the puzzle to allow novelty seeking, discussed in Chapter Nine, to be the productive trait it is for humankind. In addition to self-transcendence (the understanding that you alone aren't the center of the universe), we mentioned that novelty seeking is tempered by persistence. When we press forward in our goals and dreams in spite of obstacles in our way, we begin to delay gratification and open up our minds to greater possibilities than hollow pleasures that are right in front of our faces.

This is good news for both of you. If motivation were only ever pleasure-oriented and pain-avoidant, your partner would be out of luck, rowing up a molasses creek with nothing but a teaspoon. Watching porn is all about pleasure and pain—it's coping by drowning out the uncomfortable, boring, painful aspects of life with intense surges of pleasure.

So it works in your favor that motivation is more than that. People don't just want to survive life; they want to transcend it. They don't need life to just hand them something; they want to work to *become* something.

SACRIFICING PLEASURE TO KNOW THE TRUTH

And people will endure a lot of pain just to know what's true about the world.

Take Russians in the late '90s. I lived in Russia from '97-'98, just a few years after the Soviet Union fell. In August of '98, Russia defaulted on its national debt, and the value of the ruble plummeted. Poverty was rampant. Under communism, people weren't necessarily wealthy, but there was food on every table, warm clothes in the winter, and everyone could take a summer vacation to the Black Sea.

And now most families didn't know how they'd afford their next loaf of bread. But when I asked destitute Russians if they wished they could go back to the comforts and stability of communism, they usually told me no. Yes, life was easier then, but their government had lied to them about almost everything regarding the outside world. They'd rather live a difficult, deprived life if it meant knowing the truth about the world around them.

SACRIFICING PLEASURE TO DO THE WORK

Perhaps even more interesting, people aren't just motivated to get what they want. They want to do the work that gets them there.

Let's talk about me and Adam writing this book. We've both worked toward completing this book years longer than we planned on. It's taken hours and hours of research, interviews, rethinking and revising the entire manuscript as new data has come to light.

But if someone told either of us, "Hey, I've got this book for you, all polished and ready to go—all you have to do is slap your names on it," we would have said thanks, but no thanks. We'd take the painful process any day over a meaningless "accomplishment."

And those marathoners don't just want to shortcut to the medals and the bragging rights without running the dang thing. It's the running itself that transforms them. We want to do the work, because on some level we understand that doing the work is the only way to become someone new.

ADAM

Transcending our hedonistic, self-preserving existence sounds wonderful and inspiring, right? But let me be clear: this isn't just a pep talk about having a positive attitude. It's not about learning to believe in yourself so all your wildest dreams can come true. Understanding motivation is about knowing that every important achievement involves two changes (which we'll discuss later in this chapter):

1. A new-and-improved perspective and
2. Concrete strategies to use your energy in the right places at the right times.

Insurmountable challenges become doable when we see them through new eyes and have new tools to conquer them.

BUT WHAT IF WE'RE JUST LAZY?

So real healing and change come from rising above our pleasure-seeking, pain-avoiding selves. But transcendence is hard work. If you're not currently making progress on your transcendence trajectory, it doesn't mean that all hope is lost or that you're lazy.

The fact is, there will be times when you both may become frustrated by a seeming lack of progress, or your partner may worry that he just doesn't have the motivation necessary to take the next steps. You may even find that after finishing this book and knowing the five stones by heart, weeks or months pass and you don't take much action together to overcome porn, preferring to focus on the fun parts of your relationship instead. So how do you get past those tricky times when motivation is low?

The first step to getting out of that funk is to examine which motivations keep you stuck, because *all* behavior is motivated behavior.

In fact, did you know that there's actually no such thing as lazy? It's true. What people call "lazy" is just another motivation. Consider the girl who never agrees to go out with friends—she stays at home instead. She resists doing household tasks like dishes or laundry and prefers to get lost in a good book. She might even let a promotion pass her by at work when she could really use the raise.

Plenty of critics might call her lazy. But what if we find out that she suffers from chronic pain? She regularly experiences whole-body pain that flares up under stress, when she doesn't get enough sleep, and when she feels anxious.

In order to preserve her energy in the face of debilitating pain, she has to be careful about how she navigates life. So when friends invite her to a party, she has to consider whether feeling socially awkward might make her pain flare up. She has to think about how an hour of chores will bring all-day pain. And we can only imagine what the stress of more responsibility and pressure at work would do to her. Forget about it. So remember, choosing to avoid behaviors isn't about a lack of energy or not caring. It's about prioritizing something else entirely.

When you never quite finish that project you've been dreaming to complete forever, it might not be that you don't care enough. Maybe you care too much. Maybe your perfectionism has you paralyzed, terrified of failure. When you avoid standing up for yourself—let's say you don't ask for that raise at work—you might be motivated to avoid conflict and rejection. The guy who puts off filling out college applications could be motivated to preserve the last few months when he can feel safe under Mom and Dad's protection and resources. No matter how stuck a person looks, no matter how irrational their behavior, they're motivated to achieve a particular goal, even if they don't know it themselves.

When you understand that all behavior is motivated, it means you can do something about it. If your partner uses porn to cope instead of confront issues that could end in a fight, then his goal may be to maintain peace. If you both know that, you can figure out healthier ways to achieve that goal. So as he navigates his recovery, it will help him to examine his motivations to be where he is—because he *is* motivated to be there.

TOOLS TO BOOST MOTIVATION

Let's implement three new principles of motivation that will help you break through the tough periods we all have into growth for both yourselves and your relationship:

PRINCIPLE #1: MIND THE GAP

Here's the deal: All choices have an opportunity cost. When you want to make fundamental changes to yourself, you'll have to give up something else. In this case, your partner will give up certain behaviors that have benefited him in some way *before* the new benefits of recovery kick in. Which means there will be a gap in which he'll have no benefits at all.

For example, let's say your spending habits have landed you in enough debt to make you uncomfortable and worried. In order to get out of debt, you need to create a strict budget and stick to it. You're looking forward to the security of being debt-free. But after a few days of your debt-reduction plan, you start to feel deprived when you can't splurge on a new pair of shoes, left out when you have to turn down a lunch date with coworkers, and bored and empty after you have to cancel your Spotify. And to make matters worse, you're still weighed down by the crushing anxiety of your debt—the big number hasn't moved much yet. In order to get to the bliss of financial freedom, you're going to have to push through the pain of the gap without any benefits, new or old.

That's how it is when you make any major life change for the better. You give up one set of benefits immediately, but you'll have to keep at it consistently before you see the magnificent benefits of your new, healthy life.

Your partner will give up all of the comforts of porn as self-medication, something he may have relied on since childhood. And he'll crave those old comforts. But it may be months or more before he'll see many of the benefits of a porn-free life: a closer, more trusting relationship with you, improved moods, a clearer mind, total transparency about his life, etc. It's not unlike organizing your pantry, when the disaster on your shelves becomes an even bigger disaster on your kitchen counter before you streamline everything into a tidy masterpiece. It has to get worse before it can get better.

In fact, thousands of men who give up porn and then write about their experiences on late neurologist Gary Wilson's website yourbrainonporn.com report a period of what they call a "flatline." For the weeks or months after quitting porn and masturbation, their sex drive plummets and they experience zero desire for partnered sex. But the ones who stick it out report a "reboot"—the ability to have a healthy, intimate sex life where their brains are no longer wired to respond solely to sex on a screen.

You'll experience your own gap in benefits as the two of you work together to keep porn from invading your relationship. If you have a habit of taking control of situations to improve them, it may be a struggle at first as you allow your partner to make his own decisions. You'll need to mind the gap when you're frustrated about not seeing immediate sobriety or if he's not digging as deep into recovery as you want him to. In those situations, it's much easier to jump in and take over. But that won't help in the long run. And this in-between time may make you feel uncomfortable or helpless.

So as you work together to overcome a pornography habit, it will be easier to maintain momentum if you're both aware of the gap between giving up the old, comfortable benefits before the life-changing new ones kick in.

PRINCIPLE #2: REINTERPRET OBSTACLES

In your battle to overcome porn, you'll naturally encounter obstacles along the way. For example, relapses happen, and they can sometimes feel devastating. It's easy to fixate on the relapse, wondering what went wrong and how you can safeguard yourselves against another one. You may even begin to obsess about them, believing if you can just figure out the right filter to use, the time of day or environment that leads to relapse, or the perfect set of tools to combat them, you can cut future relapses off at the pass. Or relapses may just make one or both of you want to throw in your matching monogrammed towels.

WENDY

But here's what Tory Higgins, professor of business and psychology at Columbia University, has to say about roadblocks: fixating on obstacles in our path decreases our motivation and throws us off-course, heading straight for disaster. But he's found another, more effective approach to roadblocks.

When relapses happen (or any other obstacle that falls in your path), if you instead see them as a challenge that's a natural part of the process and focus on the goal, you'll put in more effort and find greater flow and momentum.[2] Obstacles give us the fire to fight harder if we let them.

Rats and ramps show us how this works.[3] All the way back in 1962, Leon Festinger was one of the twentieth century's most renowned social psychologists. He had pioneered the theory of cognitive dissonance and pushed the boundaries of psychological experimentation. (He once even infiltrated a doomsday cult— for science!) And then he teamed up with psychologist Douglas Lawrence to study partial reinforcement—why we continue to pursue rewards long after those rewards have disappeared.

The duo observed rats as they ran up a ramp to obtain a food reward at the top. They wanted to know if a steeper incline would deter rats from their goal. At both 25% and 50% inclines, there was no difference between the groups as long as the food remained. But when researchers removed the food, something interesting happened. You'd think the rats with the easy task of prancing up a low ramp could sustain their energy longer, hoping in vain that the food might be there this time. But it was the rats on the steeper ramp that climbed the ramp more times, looking for the missing food. Not only that, but the 50%-incline rats consistently ran *faster* than their 25%-incline counterparts, defying expectations.

ADAM

Just like those scrappy rats, when we encounter obstacles in our path, if we keep our eye on the goal, the difficulty of the task can strengthen our resolve. As you reinterpret obstacles and see the rocky path ahead as a reason to fight harder, you'll achieve more than you ever thought you would. The steeper the climb, the sweeter the victory.

Adopting this mindset will help your partner overcome his obstacles and setbacks. And reinterpreting obstacles will help you as well. There may be times when you find yourself wondering, "Is this ever going to end? Will he ever get better?" It's human to plan, to want certainty. You may find yourself in a place where you either want to know that it's all going to work out or you want to break up. If you want to see where the relationship will lead, don't run from the uncertainty. See it as a challenge. You need to live with the unknown and keep going. That uncertainty will bring you strength, empathy, endurance, perspective. We'll discuss how to live with uncertainty in Chapter Fourteen.

PRINCIPLE #3: FRONTLOAD YOUR ENERGY

When it comes down to it, motivation is really just energy. It's energy that has the power to move you from one place in life to another.

Escaping the grasp of pornography is a lot like escaping the gravitational pull of the Earth. The Earth's gravity is so powerful that it takes immense velocity and fuel to push a rocket out of our atmosphere. In fact, a rocket has to reach a velocity of seven miles per *second* to get away from Earth's gravity. This is known as *escape velocity*.

The good news for rocket scientists is that the farther away you get from Earth's mass, the less energy it takes to keep pushing you upward. Porn's pull is similar for a lot of people. It takes a *ton* of energy up front, but like gravity, the pull decreases the farther away you get.

If your partner wants to achieve escape velocity, at first he'll need a ton of fuel to propel himself away from porn's seductive pull. Using all of that energy may feel mentally exhausting. It will seem very time- and attention-consuming. He needs to know that it will get easier. Once he reaches escape velocity, a little effort goes a long way. The further away from compulsive porn use he gets, the easier it gets to avoid falling back.

So much of life takes longer than we think it should—home improvement projects, term papers, recovering from loss, learning a new skill. As Hofstadter's Law elegantly predicts, "Everything always takes longer than you expect, even when you take into account Hofstadter's Law." It's funny because it's true.

So when the process of making it beyond Earth's gravitational pull seems unending, it's important to understand that even though you both might feel like he'll be doing this forever, at some point, recovery will become second nature to him. He won't always have to apply the energy and will that he does right now.

Frontloading energy looks something like this:

Early in his recovery process, your future husband may be attending recovery meetings one or more times per week, calling group members or other support people up to several times a day, attending personal or couples counseling as needed on a weekly basis, creating and following relapse-prevention plans when he's feeling triggered, and generally putting in the level of work you'd expect from someone who's tackling porn recovery like it's his part-time job.

This is especially true if his porn use has been frequent and compulsive for a large part of his life. It might seem like overkill, but for him, it may not be. It's all about getting enough momentum going so that when he slows down his efforts, he doesn't come crashing back into a massive porn relapse.

Staying motivated through a long-haul healing process is not an easy task. But it's also not impossible. Being mindfully aware of the gap of delayed gratification between old and new benefits, seeing challenges and obstacles in your way as opportunities for growth, and frontloading your energy will help the two deal with the inevitable grind that any formidable task requires.

WHERE ARE YOU? Our session starts in ten minutes!
I'm coming. I'm just making sure Cara knows how to use the register.

Genevieve closes the text window and taps her restless fingers on her phone as the heat blasts through the car, straining to keep out the Minnesota winter. Will Jacob ever come out?

Minutes pass before Jacob runs to the car, his eyes barely visible between his scarf and hat. He opens the driver's side, and Genevieve slides over to the passenger seat, folding her arms over her chest. The car creeps out of the icy parking lot and down the empty street, veering all over the road each time they hit an invisible patch of ice.

"We're going to be so late!" Genevieve groans.

"Everyone is running late in these conditions. Daryl will understand."

"Darren."

"Yeah. Whatever."

"Jacob, why can't you make these appointments a priority?"

"What do you mean? I'm the one who called three different babysitters to find one to watch the kids!"

"Yeah, but that doesn't help if we're late!"

"Genevieve, Cara was late too. I had to train her today. I can't just leave her at the bookstore and hope she doesn't burn it down."

"Yeah, but you didn't have to schedule her for today."

"I didn't know it was going to snow!"

"You could have checked the weather!"

Jacob lets out a groan and pumps the brakes as they barely miss sliding into a parked car on the curb. "I don't know how to do anything right for you!"

"I just want you to care, Jacob! It's not that hard!"

"What are you even talking about? I got an MBA for YOU! I run a bookstore because that's what YOU wanted! We bought a house for YOU! I'm going to counseling for YOU! We switched therapists because YOU didn't like the last one!"

"Yeah, well she didn't get us at all. She kept telling me to leave you if you didn't stop watching porn!" Genevieve looks out the window, her chest tight.

Jacob pulls into a parking spot. 1:08 PM. Eight minutes late, and they still have to make it inside. In one movement, Genevieve opens the door, jumps out of the car, and slides onto the ice, butt-first. Ouch. In the space of a second Jacob is there, arm extended, eyes worried.

Genevieve looks around, relieved to see no spectators, and laughs. She lets Jacob take her hand to help her up, then takes it back and dusts herself off and starts walking.

"Anyway, she just didn't get us."

Jacob nods, hands in his pockets now. "Yeah."

He stops for a second, looking at Genevieve sidewise out of the corner of his eye. "I fixed the books—I found the $8.93."

Genevieve's eyes widen. "You did? Where was it?"

"It was applied to the wrong vendor," Jacob says. "It went on Robert Wilson's account instead of Robert Westover's. Too many Robert W's in the system."

"I was up 'til two working on that last night! Why didn't you tell me?"

Jacob shrugs. "I tried to. You were so angry at me. That's why I was late. It took me an hour and a half, and I had to write an algorithm that the software doesn't have, but I found it. And I trained Cara." He gives Genevieve half a smile.

Genevieve hesitates, then reaches out for his hand as they walk into the building, past a circa-1980s Honda Civic. Genevieve points, "Hey, look. Your old car. The Kraken."

Jacob squeezes her hand.

Jacob replays the events of last week as he sits with Genevieve on Darren's couch, legs touching. Here we go again: Jacob pretending to be the perfect husband, Genevieve trying to hold her tongue. They'll both talk circles around the near-constant angst and despair, even though Darren says they're supposed to be *so vulnerable* in his office. As if that weren't pure recklessness. In the car afterward is when it always gets bad. Only then do the words with fangs and claws start flying between them.

"The thing is, Genevieve gets upset about me using porn. I get that. She should be. But she also freaks out about these tiny things, these normal problems that couples have. And she treats me like I'm always going behind her back, even when I'm just trying to do the right thing. I mean, Daryl, you know— "

Genevieve rolls her eyes. "It's Darren."

"It's actually Derek," Darren says.

"Oh," Jacob and Genevieve reply in unison.

"Jinx." Jacob winks at Genevieve.

Genevieve grunts, eyeing Derek. "See? He's doing it again! He's pretending to be so chill. Like he has zero problems. He's making me out to be the bad guy, the one that needs all the help!"

"That seems to really bother you," Derek says.

"Well, yeah! He can't even quit looking at porn, not for more than a few days, even when he promises not to. And then he begs me to forgive him. And he always says I'm overreacting any time I'm emotional about anything, when I have a right to be upset! And he picks fights with me too. But nobody sees that! Everyone just thinks he's Mr. Perfect! The other day we went over to see my parents, and he pretended to be Mr. Nice Guy the entire time. It ruined the whole day!"

Derek rests his hand on his chin and crosses his legs. "Genevieve, why do you give him so much power?"

"What?" Genevieve thinks for a second. "What do you mean? We're married. We have kids together. He's the most important person in my life. I need him to be there for us."

"That's true. But what if he never gets better? Will you let that ruin your whole life?"

Genevieve grinds her teeth and narrows her eyes at Darren-Derek. "I don't think you understand what I'm saying. I'm not just angry because he's looking at porn. How can he be invested in us when he's keeping secrets from me and giving all this attention to someone else? To some*thing* else?"

Jacob breaks through. "Genevieve, I do love you. I care about you, the kids, the bookstore, everything we have."

Genevieve looks away.

"Why do you think I don't love you just because I have problems?" Jacob asks.

Tears well, and Genevieve breathes them back down. "If you love me, then why do you keep hurting me?" All those sleepless nights, the fights after the truth came out, the past twenty months of marital hell, the counseling that was supposed to help but only seemed to make everything worse, the growing distance between them that makes Genevieve feel frantic and adrift.

Derek's voice cuts through the air, "Well, maybe you should think about whether or not you want to be in a relationship with someone who isn't invested."

Genevieve feels dizzy.

"It sounds like you're trying *so hard* to hold onto him."

Genevieve takes pride in never having cried in Derek's office, not after fourteen sessions, but she can't stop the tears now. "I just need him to wake up and realize what he's doing to me."

"Genevieve. I hope he does. I really do. But if he doesn't, do you want to spend the rest of your life convincing someone to love you?"

Convincing someone to love you.

Is that what she's been doing? All those fights, hoping that maybe if she insisted enough, she'd get through to him? Worrying whether Jacob would someday be the guy she needed him to be?

What if it was never supposed to be about getting through? What if...? What if Jacob wasn't the answer to her problems?

Maybe it wasn't about hanging on. That wasn't working anyway.

Maybe it was about letting go.

Jacob and Derek are talking to each other. But they sound far away. Like a TV that's been left on in an empty room.

***

Genevieve and Jacob walk in silence out into the frozen world and across the parking lot. That old Honda Civic is gone now. Genevieve doesn't take Jacob's hand this time as he follows her to the passenger-side door. He opens it and puts his hand around her waist as she climbs in.

"Don't slip."

"Uh-huh," Genevieve replies.

Jacob climbs in the driver's seat, starts the ignition, and braves the slippery ice again, his knuckles white as he grips the steering wheel.

"Do you realize that I can have a problem and still love you at the same time? You wouldn't think that an alcoholic doesn't love his wife. It's not really that different." Jacob goes on, darting glances toward Genevieve and then back at the road.

Jacob looks... on edge. How long have they lived this way, bracing themselves for disaster? When was the last time Genevieve actually relaxed? Every second of her life is earmarked, dedicated to ensuring Jacob is never out of her sight long enough to find something he shouldn't. Or allocated to agonizing about what people would think if they knew Jacob's secret. *Their* secret. Or what would happen if her kids ever found out. Or anticipating the exact moment that Jacob would leave her and life would be over. She never sleeps through the night, not even when Maya and Owen do. And she wakes every morning crushed by fear. It isn't a life.

"Are you okay?" Jacob asks, coming back into focus.

"Huh? Oh. Yeah."

"You just seem... I don't know. What do you think about what Daryl said?"

"Darren. No— Derek."

"That's what I meant."

Genevieve watches the icicles hanging from the businesses they pass, dripping water frozen in time. Across the street, children play in a snowdrift.

Maybe... Maybe she and Jacob won't work out. Who knows, maybe they just *can't*. But then again, maybe they will. They might still live happily ever after someday.

But she's tired of trying to force it.

"I just realized... I realized that if you really didn't want to be in the marriage, I don't think I would want you to stay. I wouldn't want to be married to someone who doesn't want to be married to me." Genevieve can hardly believe the words that are spilling out of her mouth.

"Well, I do love you and I want to be mar—"

"And if you choose to never get better, I'll be okay without you."

Jacob's eyes widen. "Without me?"

Genevieve inhales into her belly, which feels hollow like a sort of chasmic loss. Empty, and somehow soothing too.

"It's so funny. How many times have I heard it? How many times have you told me that the porn was your demon, that it had nothing to do with me? And all those times a therapist told us that you can't *make* me happy? Maybe it just clicked."

"Wait— Genevieve?"

"I'm strong. I made it through my crazy family. I need to learn to be happy on my own."

It feels right as she says it. It feels new.

"On your own?" Jacob's face is white. "Genevieve, are we okay?"

"Yeah. We're good."

Snow is falling again, coating the world in pure quiet.

"We're good."

1   Higgins, Tory E. *Beyond Pleasure and Pain: How Motiva-*
     tion Works. New York: Oxford University Press, 2012.

2   Higgins, Tory E. *Beyond Pleasure and Pain: How Motiva-*
     tion Works. New York: Oxford University Press, 2012.

3   Lawrence, Douglas H., and Leon Festinger. "Deterrents
     and Reinforcement: The Psychology of Insufficient
     Reward." *American Psychological Association.* Stanford:
     Stanford University Press, 1962.

14. STONE #5:
CARING FOR YOURSELF

*Breathe. Let go. And remind yourself that this very moment is the
only one you know you have for sure.*
  —*Oprah Winfrey*

WENDY

In the end, I interviewed about a dozen women who were affected
by a partner's porn use, women I could divide into three general
categories. Some of them hadn't yet experienced much trauma
about their partner's compulsions, and maybe they never would.
Others were still in the throes of trauma, wondering if life would
ever get better. And then some women could recall the trauma
they once felt, the way it took over their lives and identity, thinking
they'd never feel normal again. But by the time I spoke to them,
they seemed self-assured and, dare I say it, happy. Their trauma
was a distant memory.

There isn't a one-size-fits-all, universal path to healing from
trauma. Everyone has to find their own way. And each woman I
spoke with seemed to have found it through different means and
in their own timing. But they all had one thing in common. Each of

them told me, "I eventually realized that his porn use had nothing to do with me."

Knowledge is power, and this knowledge packs a neutron bomb's worth of it. Knowing that you don't have a role in your partner's compulsions means you don't ever have to take responsibility for his pornography use, thinking things would be different if you'd only done something different. It means you don't have to feel like you're not pretty enough, not thin enough, not nice enough, not sexual enough—his porn habit has nothing to do with any of that. It's likely been with him since long before he met you. And even though we've filled this book with plenty of ways you can help him out and understand what he's experiencing, when it comes down to it, it's his job to overcome his problems.

And even though you might intellectually understand this, it may take you a while to truly internalize that his porn use has nothing to do with you. While you're on that path, you'll need to take steps to keep yourself sane. Take care of yourself in three key ways: by understanding your pain, setting healthy boundaries, and practicing self-care.

UNDERSTANDING YOUR OWN PAIN

ADAM

Emotional pain can be quite unpredictable. A few years into our marriage, we lost our first baby fourteen weeks into my wife's pregnancy. We both count it as the most painful experience of our lives. And even though it happened over a decade ago, the pain still hits me unexpectedly sometimes. Sometimes I spend an hour or so grieving, crying, and sharing my pain. And then I'll go a year without thinking much about our lost son. And just when I think I've worked through all of those emotions of grief and loss, they pop back up again, just as powerful as they ever were.

Our emotions change. No feeling is permanent. Remember, married women are much more likely than unmarried ones to be traumatized by discovering a partner's porn use, so even if you aren't feeling distress now, be prepared for the unexpected.

If you do end up distressed or even traumatized during your

significant other's recovery journey, you'll need to take care of yourself by healing your wounds. And in order to do that, you need to figure out what those wounds are. Of course his porn use hurts you. It takes him away from everything that matters in life. It objectifies and dehumanizes women. It feels like an emotional betrayal when he gives his time and energy to another woman, even if she's an image on a screen. That energy should be reserved for you.

But if your distress when he uses pornography feels more intense than you expected or more all-consuming than the reasons we've listed above—if it feels like a visceral, personal attack on you—this may mean there's more going on underneath.

This type of extreme distress often means there's a compounding issue, as we discussed briefly at the end of Chapter Two. For example, maybe you went into marriage fearing that your imperfect body wouldn't be attractive to your husband. You grew up with the all-too-common body loathing that plagues plenty of women. Your parents regularly commented on your weight and appearance. You've worried about this since puberty. Discovering your partner's secret porn use suddenly confirmed that your body is unacceptable. That your partner is more attracted to other women. That you aren't enough.

That's just one potential example, but the point is, when you're feeling intense distress, something that feels similar has happened to you before, and there's a synergistic effect—the whole is more than the sum of its parts. When we surprise ourselves by reacting in intense ways, we may be recalling issues that are much, much older than our current struggle, often dating back to our most formative years.[1]

Whether you had loving, attentive parents doing the best they could with what they had or if you were a latchkey kid who was tossed from foster home to foster home, childhood can simply be traumatic. Parents are often overwhelmed and always imperfect. Kids are helpless and vulnerable, and experiences that may seem insignificant to adults can feel world-ending to children. They haven't yet been given any tools or perspective to deal with all of the pain, heartbreak, anger, and lonely moments of life. And the traumas of childhood can have far-reaching effects into adulthood. So if your response to his porn use feels extreme or overwhelming, or if it becomes overwhelming if he relapses later on, it may be because of one of the following underlying childhood wounds, identified by psychologist Francine Shapiro:[*2]

DEFECTIVENESS

Maybe you feel that your partner's pornography use means you aren't enough for him. As a kid you came to believe you weren't acceptable, and that has persisted into your adult relationships.

LACK OF SAFETY

Your childhood was unsafe or lacked stability in one or more ways. Thus, you feel increased anxiety that his pornography use puts your relationship in danger.

LACK OF AUTONOMY OR CONTROL

As a child, you were given little control over your own life. Your choices and desires didn't matter. Now you feel like the chaos of life just happens to you, that you don't have a voice, and you have neither the right nor the resources to confront your problems.

RESPONSIBILITY

You had too much responsibility heaped upon your shoulders as a child. Or you had a tendency to feel that everything bad that happened was somehow your fault. Now you believe his recovery is your job, and you feel responsible for all of his slips and relapses, almost as if you caused them.

Just about every emotional distress a human can feel can be placed into one of the above categories. Upset that you didn't get into the college you wanted to? You're probably feeling defective or broken. Your partner on a school project isn't doing anything

---

* Francine Shapiro, the creator of EMDR therapy, has proposed that all of our issues boil down to four underlying wounds that originate in childhood and persist into adulthood.

to help you finish, and you're desperate to maintain your 4.0 GPA? Responsibility. Your supervisor at work has unreasonable expectations of you, but you don't feel like you have the right to stick up for yourself? Lack of control. You quadruple-check that you locked all the doors at night before going to bed? Safety.

These themes usually present themselves earlier in life (often because of your family's dynamics and behavior) and pop up throughout the rest of it. You start to believe they're true. You start to watch for them, predict them, and then look for evidence that indeed, you are worthless or the world is dangerous. So even though it's naturally upsetting when your partner hides his porn use, it's often compounded pain from unresolved issues. You worry that he doesn't really love you and would rather spend time with a person on a screen? That's defectiveness. You know what he needs to do to change, but you feel like no one will listen to you? Control. You feel that if he doesn't change, it will be because you failed him personally? Responsibility. You're terrified this means the end of your relationship? Safety.

The fact is, you may be dealing with much larger issues than you realized. And these issues won't resolve themselves overnight or on their own. As you examine the underlying pain and trauma in your life, you'll need some tools to help you make it through each day. You'll need to set firm boundaries and practice self-care.

SETTING BOUNDARIES

Boundaries are a paradox that many people misunderstand. People often see them as harsh and selfish. Sometimes it might seem like boundaries will keep you from having an intimate relationship. But in reality, boundaries are at the heart of all stable relationships.

Let me show you what I mean: When my wife and I moved into our neighborhood, no one had fences because all of the homes were new. People started putting trampolines, basketball hoops, fire pits, and even a swimming pool in their backyards. Our neighbors were amicable, and everyone was excited about making friendships. A couple of neighbors suggested that we all forego the whole fence issue so that everyone could share everyone else's toys. They wanted to build a little suburban utopia. Sounds lovely, right?

But something didn't sit quite right with Lindsay and me about this idea. We were mulling it over one day when a down-the-street neighbor, an attorney, dropped by. We both surveyed my backyard, and he said, "You know what that in-ground trampoline is called to an attorney? An attractive nuisance. If you leave it open for anyone's use and someone gets hurt, you can be held liable. You should put in a fence."

So we installed that fence. And everyone else followed suit. And the funny thing is, having fences has helped to *protect* our neighborly relationships. Instead of us feeling used when random kids jump on our trampoline when we'd like a little privacy, or the pool owners feeling like they need to monitor their pool day and night to make sure no one drowns, we can share with neighbors on our own terms. The neighborhood kids still come knocking on our door to play with our children, we host a neighborhood barbecue in the summer, and we love the friendships that have grown in our neighborhood. But we know where to draw the line.

The same goes with marriages. Even though boundaries are by definition a way of creating distance between two or more people (whether emotional, social, or physical), they can also be the best way to save your sanity, help you avoid being taken advantage of, and create the safety you need to be able to build strong bonds.

Some examples of healthy boundaries in a typical marriage:

- A rule about not making significant purchases without consulting each other
- An agreement that both spouses will be responsible for the housework
- A commitment to not maintain active, close friendships with ex-girlfriends or boyfriends

This last example relates to how you'll set boundaries with regard to your partner's ongoing porn struggles. Some marriages have a sort of "don't ask, don't tell" agreement when it comes to pornography, like it's none of the wife's business, so she should just ignore it as long as her husband doesn't ask her to get involved.

You'll need to set boundaries if you want to create a different type of marriage than that.

Setting boundaries might feel new and potentially scary to you. In that case, you may need to practice or get help setting boundaries at first. Remember, boundaries aren't demands or consequences. They aren't manipulation or punishment. They're statements about what you expect from your relationship and what you'll do to protect it when it's in danger. Boundaries ensure you're taking care of yourself and your marriage.

WENDY

For example, when Penny (the one who had attended Adam's lecture about dating a pornography user) was first dating Edwin (whose fiancée had ghosted him after he wasn't forthcoming about his pornography use), he was seeking out porn every day, as he had since he was twelve. He started attending twelve-step meetings after he met Penny, but he was making zero progress with abstinence from porn, despite the fact that Penny had communicated how important this was to her.

For weeks, Edwin even maintained that he was going to start step two, which involved a good bit of introspection and some writing. One weekend he told Penny that this was it—he was definitely going to start writing step two. Penny decided to give him time to do so, so she made other plans with her sister for the weekend. When Penny met Edwin for lunch on Monday and learned he still hadn't started step two and instead watched movies all day Saturday, she was disappointed. She felt like she and Edwin were going nowhere.

So she made a choice. It wasn't an easy one. Heartbroken, she told Edwin that she couldn't see him anymore until he'd been sober for six months and had completed step four (which is to make a complete written inventory of how your compulsions have harmed yourself and others).

Now here's the thing: in Penny's case, her decision wasn't manipulation. She wasn't trying to punish Edwin. She was devastated to break up with him, knowing full well that she might never see him again. She liked him *a lot*. But she also knew she was selling herself short by staying with a guy who paid lip service to meeting her needs but wasn't willing to walk the walk. Penny wasn't trying to manufacture a certain outcome. She had no clue what might happen next. She was simply protecting herself from a relationship in which she continually made requests that went ignored.

Let me be clear: Setting boundaries won't make a person change according to your wishes. You set boundaries for your own well-being while understanding that you can't control another person's choices.

This could easily have been the end of Penny and Edwin's story, but it wasn't. When Penny broke up with Edwin, it was a wake-up call for him. He achieved six months of sobriety and completed step four, all while Penny and Edwin had no contact. She dated a little bit in the meantime. But when Edwin contacted Penny after those six months, she was overjoyed. They could be together again, now that Edwin had a new sober life.

Penny's boundaries were about her own well-being, allowing herself the freedom to stay out of the drama of Edwin's struggle. Regardless of Edwin's choices, Penny did what she needed to do for her own mental health.

ADAM

The fact is, your partner needs your influence in his life, whether he knows it yet or not. The research says that it's often husbands who can make or break a marriage, *depending on whether or not they accept their wives' influence*.[3] So be honest with him, communicate your feelings and apprehensions, and allow yourself to be a force for good in his life. If he's smart, he'll take all that to heart.

Many books have been written about the complexity of boundaries. I've listed a few for you to refer to in Appendix D. But let me give you a starting point, based on changes I see other people making for their own healing.

As patient and forgiving as you'll want to be with your new relationship, your partner may sometimes engage in behaviors that require you to set boundaries to protect what you are building together. (Of course, you won't necessarily set boundaries any time you feel upset or hurt or don't like something, because if your policy is to shut down the relationship any time you feel hurt, you'll often find yourself disappointed about being married to a mere mortal.)

With regard to pornography use, wives often report these behaviors from a husband to be the most painful or difficult to deal with:

- Continually lying about his porn use
- Manipulating her into believing that his porn use is her fault
- Refusing to discuss his porn use at all
- Failure to take any steps toward change
- Getting involved in porn that is illegal, disturbing, or involves real human interaction

Most women I've worked with understand that their partners have relied on their porn use for a long time, and it isn't going to disappear overnight. They know that compulsions take time and work to overcome. Because of this, you may set an early boundary around honesty. As long as your partner tells the truth about his struggles, you can stay invested in the relationship—even if the truth is that he's relapsing more often than either of you would like. This is the most common boundary my clients set at the beginning of therapy. The rest of the above issues may also require a firm boundary. Nobody should have to endure damaging behaviors like lying, manipulation, and disrespect.

In these cases, consider setting abrupt boundaries like time apart or a serious conversation about the status of the relationship. As in all things, use judgment and get feedback if you need it. A well-placed boundary can redirect a relationship that is off course.

WENDY

Boundaries actually create space to stay in your relationship *and* make sure your needs are met. They open up a certain kind of space called *liminal space*. Liminal spaces are uncomfortable, ambiguous spaces, where we've started down a path, but haven't yet arrived at our destination. They're the stretch of time that exists between the strike of twelve when your coach becomes a pumpkin and the moment when the missing glass slipper slides on your foot.

When I first met Alex, she was a twenty-three-year-old undergrad with long, blonde hair and tie-dye leggings. She was in a long-term relationship with Luke. They'd started out as friends. Luke had been upfront with Alex about his compulsive porn use before they were even dating. Alex decided she liked Luke's honesty and the way he seemed kind and authentic around her, unlike the other guys she'd dated. And she and Luke had a certain chemistry, so after a few months of "just friends," they started dating.

Fast-forward eighteen months, and Alex would have loved to get engaged, but Luke was still struggling to be mentally well and fully present for Alex. Luke had actually managed three months abstinence from pornography by the time I met Alex, but he was still masturbating compulsively. And what troubled Alex more, he was letting his chronic depression get the best of him. During that time, Luke was fired from two jobs because he wouldn't show up to work if he was going to be late or if he was in an emotional funk. The idea of arriving to work in a less-than-perfect state caused Luke a lot of anxiety. Some days Luke would sleep all day long in an attempt to avoid life.

On Alex's part, she had a lot of anxiety of her own about marrying a man who couldn't hold down a job or fully function in society. And she'd been engaged once before to a man who was clinically depressed, which hadn't worked out and had left her heartbroken. Plus, she was worried that her family wouldn't understand why she would date a compulsive porn user, if they ever found out Luke's secrets. But at the same time, over the eighteen months she'd dated Luke, she'd come to love him, and the idea of breaking up devastated her. Alex felt stuck in no-man's-land. She longed for the security of knowing whether things would work out for them or not. And if not, she could just cut ties, stop spinning her wheels, *and* avoid any more pain.

But she ended up finding comfort in the idea of liminal spaces.

She first learned about them in an English class, but they're a concept borrowed from anthropology, from the study of rite-of-passage rituals in different cultures.

Take the Maasai people, the fierce, red-robed warriors from East Africa. That path to warriorhood isn't easy. Young boys live a life of play, but when they reach ten to fourteen years of age, they begin the ceremony that initiates them into the warrior class. First, an initiant herds cattle alone for seven days. When he returns home, he's circumcised without anesthesia the next morning at dawn. He wears black while he heals over the next four to eight months, after which he's welcomed into the warrior's camp.

But after all that, he's still not yet a warrior. He must live and train in the warrior's camp for *ten years* before he can rejoin society, and only then will he be a senior warrior. Throughout those ten years, he must be able to make a life for himself in that liminal space, no longer a boy, but not yet a man nor a full-fledged warrior.

Ten years is a long time to live in that in-between space. It brought Alex comfort to realize that in cultures the world over, people exist in liminal spaces, having not yet arrived at the place they want to be. One day, when she found herself in the midst of a panic attack, she began to repeat a mantra that helped her make sense of her situation: "This is not about disaster. This is about choice. There is pain in both decisions. There is no easy way." That mantra helped her through each day with an unknown future ahead.

ADAM

Setting boundaries with your partner creates liminal space for both of you. It can be an uncomfortable space, because you're trying to create change but haven't yet mastered the healthy dynamic you want. It isn't the space itself that causes healing. Liminal space creates *opportunity* to heal and allows you to be patient in the transition. To quote Robert Frost, often there's "no way out but through."[4]

A boundary can help keep you from going back to the way things were when you don't yet know what the new normal looks like. According to Franciscan friar Richard Rohr, "Boundaries seem to be the only way that human beings can find a place to stand, a place to begin, a place from which to move out."[5] Setting boundaries can help you two stay together without compromising your own needs and expectations. In this way, a boundary is a statement of hope about the future.

Living in uncertain spaces is part of being human—when you're a penniless grad student who began your program months ago but still have years of grueling study before you'll be able to call yourself a doctor. Or when you've experienced miscarriage after miscarriage, and you'll just have to wait and see if this is the pregnancy that will grant you a healthy child. When someone you love receives a cancer diagnosis, and you'll just have to wait to know if they'll pull through. Most of our lives are spent in spaces where we've begun a process but haven't yet seen it through. Growth happens as you cross the impossible chasm, not in the comfort of the other side.

WENDY

Two months after I spoke with Alex that first time, Luke drove her out to a lovely field at sunset and proposed marriage. The gentle breeze and the warm sunshine made for the perfect romantic setting. Alex said no.

Luke had told his closest friends that he was planning to propose, and that he and Alex would either come home from their magical evening engaged or broken up. Neither of these options transpired. Alex told Luke that she loved him very much and thanked him for the thoughtful proposal. She let him know that she wanted to keep on dating, but she couldn't say yes right now. She wouldn't feel right promising to marry him yet. Alex was learning to trust her gut. And her gut told her that she needed to stay in that liminal space for now, even though she longed for answers and resolution.

She drew on what she learned from her twelve-step group for partners, and she started to set up boundaries. "That changed everything," Alex later told me. "I realized that boundaries gave me power. Not power to manipulate Luke, but power over my anxiety. I no longer had to worry all the time whether I was making the right choice marrying Luke or not marrying him, or worrying what my family might think of me if they knew I was dating a porn addict, because I was making the right choices for myself, and that helped me feel safe."

EXAMPLES OF BOUNDARIES

ADAM

Like Alex, you may find yourself in a place where your relationship isn't making progress, but you don't want to break up, either. Sometimes you just feel stuck. In these cases, healthy boundaries expose the problem and create space for new solutions. Let's show you some examples of how to set a boundary:

EXAMPLE #1: SETTING A BOUNDARY WHEN THERE'S TOO LITTLE PROGRESS

When you're just getting started, you'll both feel optimistic and hopeful. Even if your future husband has a long history of porn use, the fact that you've teamed up and have a plan will help both of you feel that you're learning and growing. But what happens if months go by and nothing has really changed? Your future husband still turns to porn with about the same frequency. He commits to stop, to do things differently, to follow the plan you two put together. But you keep on having the same conversations, he makes the same promises, and nothing seems to change.

At some point, you'll wonder if what you're doing is really working. You don't want to keep this up for the next twenty years. So a boundary makes sense here. You need to create space for him to realize that promises to change and real change aren't the same thing.

Remember, the purpose of your boundary isn't to make him change or force him to take you seriously. It exists to create space for both of you to break your current pattern. It also gives him the opportunity to stop and think about why what he's doing isn't working and take the initiative to change.

The essence of your boundary is that you need to see action.

You also won't be in charge of following up with him about it anymore. He needs to take charge of that himself.

Here's how this type of boundary might sound:

> I'm overwhelmed by feeling responsible for your recovery, and things aren't going very well. I need some space away from talking about this. Please take some time to figure out what you can change so that your recovery improves. Instead of asking you about it all the time, I'm asking you to take charge. I need to see some change so I can have hope that things won't just stay like this forever.

This boundary keeps your relationship from developing into a parent-child dynamic, which isn't very romantic. It also sets a precedent that you're not responsible for his recovery. He needs to seek out help, make changes, and ask for your feedback as he moves forward. When he gets stuck, you're there to help share ideas about what might need to change. But he's always in the driver's seat. Without a boundary like this, you'll end up being more invested than he is in his process of change—which will inevitably lead to heartache and frustration.

But what if he doesn't take charge? What if he agrees to the boundary, but doesn't make any changes? Then you'd probably sit down with him and set a second boundary after some time passes with no changes. This new boundary is about self-protection. You're in a relationship with someone who doesn't appear to understand how important this is to you. Your new boundary would make clear how you intend to respond if things continue as they are. You could say:

> I know you agreed to take charge of your recovery and healing. I've done my best to avoid stepping into a parent role with you. I also haven't seen any real change, which makes me worry about the future. I'd be happy to hear why you think you're struggling to make changes. I'm even willing to

share some ideas to try to help. But if you can't take
this seriously enough to do something different,
I'll need to take a break from our relationship to
rethink some things.

Setting this kind of boundary can be terrifying. You care about
him, and you're invested in your growing relationship. Of course
you'd only set this boundary if you'd thought it through and were
truly willing to walk away from a relationship that's harming you.
But once you've decided that his lack of change is too important to
ignore, this boundary will help him understand that if he wants to
make changes, he needs to make them now.

EXAMPLE #2: SETTING A BOUNDARY WHEN YOUR PART-
NER REFUSES TO COMMUNICATE

Conflict avoidance is another problem that can arise in a relationship
with a recovering porn user, which isn't surprising since using
porn is often the ultimate avoidance behavior for some guys.
Many of my clients are too deep in their shame to communicate
and would rather keep their problems to themselves. Or maybe
they never learned how to cope with conflict growing up. In any
event, the most common tactic is simply avoiding all discussions
about their porn use or emotionally shutting down when the topic
is brought up. This can make a partner feel like she has to do all of
the communicating.

The straight news: conflict avoiders are often the most difficult
to work with. They may very well be doing the work but don't
want to talk about it. Or they may be avoiding doing the work
and avoiding talking about it. Either way, open communication
is mission critical to a healthy marriage. It can be hard to keep a
conflict avoider in a conversation long enough to communicate
anything productive. Effective boundaries with the conflict-averse
involve three strategies:

- Let them know that you have high expectations
  for conflict engagement
- Be willing to soften the approach to the conflict (if

necessary) to keep the avoider engaged

- Often, you have to be more assertive with people who are extremely averse to conflict. If you give these types of people an option to avoid confrontation, they will take it every time. When you want to sit down and talk, be direct and explicit: "We are going to sit down and have this conversation now."

If we were to combine all three tactics into one statement, it could go something like this:

I believe that the best marriages involve open, regular communication. I know you're anxious about conflict, so I'll try to be as gentle as I can. But I'm not interested in avoiding tough topics. So I'll try to give you space to process your emotions before we talk about difficult things, but sometimes we just have to sit down and talk about this, even if you don't want to.

PRACTICE SELF-CARE

WENDY

Self-care has become a huge part of our culture these days, so much so that it's sometimes distorted to mean self-indulgence— the three-hour bubble bath while eating an entire chocolate cake, which probably means you'll be sick to your stomach and a big, wrinkled, chocolate-y mess when your bath is finished. Or taking a personal day from work when a big assignment is due soon, only to find yourself stressed and scrambling to present a subpar project at the last minute.

What self-care really is: taking time for yourself to transform into a healthier, more functional, more at-peace human being. It's taking a hike in the hills to get your blood flowing and reflect on the wonders of nature. It's enrolling in a class just for fun so you can learn a new skill. It's practicing meditation to calm your mind and learn to be present with your emotions. It's also turning off Netflix so you can get your project done. It's going to bed when you're tired, so you can get a full night's rest. It's eating your leafy greens. It's making that doctor's appointment.

ADAM

Three general types of self-care will benefit you as you navigate recovery together with your future husband: emotional, physical, and spiritual.

EMOTIONAL SELF-CARE

Emotional self-care involves letting yourself feel your feelings without judging them or drowning in the intensity of those emotions. It's also being honest about your feelings with your significant other *and* with yourself. It's being patient with your humanity, allowing yourself to make mistakes, to be messy, and still maintain a growth mindset. Hearkening back to Chapter One, just because you haven't yet transformed into the person you want to be doesn't mean that you can't.

PHYSICAL SELF-CARE

Your physical well-being often informs your emotional and relational well-being. Ever tried to have a productive discussion with a hangry person? Ever been hangry yourself? Yeah. I've been there too. When we aren't feeling great physically, it's hard to make progress in any other areas of our lives. This boils down to resource management. When we're low on resources, we struggle to respond in the ways we want to.

So get your body moving. Eat a balanced diet. Put your phone away and prioritize sleep. Practice mindfulness and meditation to manage your stress. It's not about being perfect; it's about making small improvements and feeling their benefits. Your body will thank you, but so will your overall well-being.

SPIRITUAL SELF-CARE

Antoine de Saint-Exupéry once said (popularly paraphrased here), "If you want to build a ship, don't drum up people together to collect wood and don't assign them tasks and work, but rather teach them to long for the endless immensity of the sea."[6] Spiritual self-care is about the big picture. It's finding meaning in your existence, understanding that you have intrinsic value, that you have something to contribute to make society a better place.

Ways to practice spiritual self-care:

- Meditation or prayer
- Reflecting on the purpose of your existence
- Making a meaningful contribution to the lives of others
- Bonding with others about our shared human experience
- Connecting with creation through nature

No one can take better care of you than you can. Whether you're confronting pornography, financial stresses, parenting issues, illness, a stressful work environment, aging parents, devastating losses, or any of the thousands of challenges that couples face, having the powerful tools of self-awareness, boundaries, and self-care will provide you the strength and resilience to be present for those struggles.

JACOB   JUNE 2015

Jacob is doing great. Thirty-six days now.

With Maya on one knee, Owen on the other, Jacob declares, "Theeee end," for the sixth time this evening and closes the torn-up copy of *The Three Little Pigs*.

"Again, Daddy!" Owen shouts.

Jacob shakes his head, setting the book on the kitchen table.

"Later."

The garage door swings wide open, then back, stopping with a thud just before it closes. Genevieve's leg pushes it slowly open again. Then the rest of Genevieve emerges, lugging a stack of cardboard boxes.

"Hey! Let me get those." Jacob jumps up, setting Maya and Owen down in one movement, pulling the boxes from Genevieve's arms. "You're not supposed to move anything heavy."

Genevieve snickers. "I pick up Owen all the time, and these don't weigh half what he does."

"But still... Just take it easy, okay?"

"These baby girl clothes have been sitting in our garage since we moved here."

"But what if it's a boy?" He imagines Owen holding a baby brother, big and proud and beaming, no longer the little caboose.

"Still, no harm in unpacking boxes that have been gathering dust for eighteen months." Genevieve smiles, pursing her lips. "Anyway, it's a girl. Lily."

She rubs her belly, which hasn't yet started to grow.

Genevieve walks down the hall toward their bedroom, Jacob following with the boxes. He sets them on the floor and opens one, laying the clothes out on the bed. Genevieve does the same.

"Hey! Guess what tonight is?" Jacob starts in.

Genevieve examines a pink-striped onesie, rubbing at a stain with her thumb. "Umm, what? Oh, wait—your meeting. You gotta get going."

She reaches into the box for another stack of clothes.

Jacob inhales, his chest growing. "It's my big day! My thirty-day chip!"

Owen wanders in, holding his book high above his head like a salute.

"We'll read it later, Buddy," Genevieve responds. Owen turns around and walks back out.

"So... yeah. thirty-day chip." Jacob starts again. "Actually thirty-six, if you're counting."

Genevieve nods, smoothing the bunched-up ruffle of a tiny skirt.

"That's good. I hope it's helping you." She's still staring at the skirt, frowning at the noncompliant ruffle.

"Genevieve, it's the longest I've gone. Thirty-six days. I think I'm finally figuring this out, after all this time."

Genevieve looks up, seeing him now and giving him a half-smile. "I do hope it's helping. I'm happy for you. I know you've really wanted this."

Jacob's smile slackens. "Yeah, I have. For us." He moves toward Genevieve.

She waves him away. "Then hurry up! Don't be late on your big day!" she smiles, walking out of the room.

"Okay! Don't lift any more boxes!" Jacob calls down the hall.

But she's already gone.

Right. Onto the meeting. Jacob gives Maya and Owen two hugs apiece (plus a bonus hug for a forlorn Owen when he follows Jacob out to the garage), grabs the keys to the 4Runner, their first respectable, shiny, white-picket-fence vehicle, and starts his drive into the city that he's made twice a week for the past four months now. He reaches for the stereo, but stops, driving a while in silence, bathing in the moody colors of the setting sun.

All he and Genevieve ever used to do was fight. About the porn, yes. But about everything else, too. Every single thing he did seemed to upset her. He could never figure out her rules.

But now... Now that she's all zen... Now that she's somehow fallen out of his orbit... It's good, right?

He tugs his collar away from his neck.

He parks outside of the public library and grabs a paper napkin from the passenger seat to wipe a bit of soot from the hood of the 4Runner on his way in. A dingy red Nissan Sentra rattles right up next to Jacob's car. A scruffy man in a plaid work shirt gets out, waving to Jacob on his way into the building.

"Hey, Jacob."

Jacob nods back, hands in his pockets. He sees the familiar faces of some other men as they funnel into the building.

When Jacob gets to the basement, the scruffy man is already sitting in the circle. Jacob considers the open chair next to him, but decides on a wide, empty spot and sits down on the cold metal chair.

Time ticks by as the other men chat and take their seats. Carl calls the meeting to order and reads through the opening script. Jacob taps his foot as various men share, the raw rhythm of their tragic, hopeful stories all blending into one.

As one guy in a backward baseball cap finishes, no more than a kid, and the crowd murmurs their thank yous, Jacob leans forward and clears his throat.

"Hi. I'm Jacob. I'm a sex addict."

"Hi, Jacob," the room replies.

Jacob inhales.

"Guys, I'm getting my thirty-day chip today. I mean, it's actually been thirty-six days. We just didn't meet last Monday because of the holiday. I know that's nothing, really—not much compared to the sobriety some of you have. But I'm on my way. These last thirty-six days have opened my eyes. I realized that I wasn't taking recovery seriously before. But I'm managing my internet access now. I've set up filters. I moved my computer to a public area in my house. And if I'm bored, I just choose not to use the internet at all because that's a major risk for me."

Jacob pauses, glancing around the room. The boy in the backwards cap nods at him.

"And I've started writing again! I started a brand-new book. Brand-new book, brand-new life. I haven't written in *years*. I don't know why I let so much time slip away. But whatever—spilled milk and all that, right? I'm crossing a threshold.

"I'm learning I have to set a goal to make things happen. It's all about mindset. I set a thirty-day goal, and it worked! And now I have a ninety-day goal, and we're just gonna go from there."

Backwards-cap boy nods some more, eyes fixed on Jacob's. Scruffy guy is staring off into the distance, chin in his hand. Carl smiles broadly at Jacob. But if you asked Jacob, he looks more amused than inspired.

"Umm, so anyway, that's me."

"Thanks, Jacob," the crowd hums.

Jacob sits back. Carl isn't looking at him anymore. Jacob can't shake the image of Genevieve playing with the ruffle on the baby dress.

"Hi, I'm Mike," the scruffy man starts.

"Hi, Mike."

Mike exhales, his cheeks puffing.

"So it's been a hard week. My mom's been in the hospital since November. She's not doing great. But I pray every day that she can have peace, even in the middle of all the chemo and operations. The doctors are trying to save her, but it's pretty touch-and-go. None of us know what's going to happen. You can't fight that kind of thing. And thanks, everyone, all of you who texted or called this week about Mom. I feel at home here. That's one of the reasons I keep coming back year after year. You guys are family.

"Most guys my age are starting to think about retirement, but I'm just grateful to have my health so I can keep working, especially after my wife's accident. It's gotten a lot tougher at home, and we've had to make some changes in how we spend money. I get mad sometimes. Life can feel really unfair.

"I guess I'm trying to say, I didn't imagine *anything* turning out this way. But I also never thought I'd find recovery. It was under my nose the whole time, you know? It's not about me. I can't do this on my own. Help is always there. All you have to do is ask. And once I figured that out, everything started to change." Mike sits back, turns his head and scratches his ear.

"Thanks, Mike." Jacob joins the crowd.

Two more men share as the hour winds down, one of them getting animated about how he realized resentment is a trigger for him. When that's all over, Carl stands up.

"Thanks, everyone, for coming tonight. The fact that you're here is a step in the right direction. We've got a couple of chips to give out."

Carl opens his satchel and pulls out two chips.

"Jacob is getting his thirty-day chip."

Jacob stands, grinning like a spelling bee champ, and walks toward Carl.

"And Mike..."

Scruffy Mike stands as Carl fiddles with one of the chips, pushing his glasses up to examine it.

"Mike is getting his five-year chip."

The room applauds. Standing beside Mike, Jacob's smile grows stiff as Carl hands him his shiny coin.

Out in the parking lot, with his hand in his pocket, Jacob turns his chip over with his thumb and forefinger.

Baseball-cap kid passes Jacob. "Congratulations! I'm gonna get where you are."

Jacob smiles back. Then he takes a deep breath and walks up to Carl. "Hey."

Carl beams. "Well, hello, Jacob. You were supposed to call me."

"Yes! I will!" Jacob eyes Carl. "When I need help, right?"

Carl throws his head back and laughs. "Hoo, boy. You need to start figuring this out." He pats Jacob on the shoulder.

Mike's off in the distance, chatting to a man in a business suit who arrived late to the meeting.

"I had no idea he was getting his five-year chip. He never even talks about his sobriety."

"Who? Mike?" Carl asks.

"Yeah."

"Yeah, Mike's a good one," Carl replies.

Jacob kicks at some dirt. "Yeah, his story sounds pretty sad, and that's impressive that he's been sober that long, considering. I'd love to know his secret."

"His secret? He told you his secret tonight, man."

"What, you mean that stuff about asking for help? Nah, that's not what I mean. Too obvious. I mean his *real* secret."

Carl shakes his head, smiling. "Man, Jacob. You know, sometimes the right answer is still right, even if *you* don't get it."

"How do you mean?" Jacob tilts his head. Jacob had asked Carl to be his sponsor because he led the meetings and had over a decade of sobriety. He was supposed to be the best. But now here he is, giving Jacob a hard time, just because Jacob hasn't needed to call him.

"You're still too busy trusting yourself to get any real help." Carl pats him on the back and walks off, unlocking his car with his fob.

"I'm here for you, man. You gotta call me, though," Carl yells from his open window as he drives off.

The parking lot meeting is dying down. Mike walks past Jacob toward his car. He doesn't look so scruffy in the dark. "See ya, Jacob!" he yells.

"Oh! Yeah—hey! Congrats!" Jacob shouts back.

Jacob climbs in his car, sits there in the silence, letting himself sink into the seat.

Thirty-six *days*. The truth is, he's exhausted. He doesn't know how he'll make fifty-four more, let alone the rest of his life. One more week sounds impossible. Some days he feels empty, irritated for no reason, wound up. Sometimes he thinks he might die of boredom. Other days he's paralyzed by some pounding, unarticulated fear. And then for a few days the thought of porn won't even cross his mind.

On those days, he's ecstatic. Cured at last. But then the urges come back with a vengeance, and Jacob has to fight off impulse after impulse, trying in vain to fill the void with food, work, scribbling out plotlines for his new novel that go nowhere. Why can't he just choose to stop, and have that be that? Why is this, of all things, his Everest? He'd planned to be so much more than this. He's going to be a father for the third time. It's just stupid at this point. And Genevieve has actually been really cool through it all.

Genevieve.

Jacob swipes open his phone and pulls up Genevieve's number, letting his finger rest on it for a second. Then he dials.

"Jacob?"

"Hey."

"Are you all right? Everything go okay?"

"Yeah. It was good."

"Oh, that's great. You've never called me after a meeting

before. Are you driving?"

"No, I'm just sitting here in the parking lot for a minute."

"Oh. Uhh, are you all right?"

"Yeah, I'm okay. No, wait... I'm actually not."

"Okay..."

"I just... I just realized that I have no idea what I'm doing."

"What do you mean?"

"It's nothing. Well, no... I mean..."

Jacob takes a breath.

"I need help, Genevieve. I can't do this myself."

The line is silent for two long seconds.

"Jacob. I'm right here."

"No, I know, but... things seem different now. You're so... sure of yourself."

"Yeah. Well, I guess I finally realized it's not about me. Your problems, I mean. Took me long enough. My happiness doesn't have to revolve around you."

Jacob's shoulders slump. "Yeah."

"But that doesn't mean I don't love you. And I'm scared too. What if you never get better, and I have to do this on my own? I don't want that. I want to be with you."

"I *want* to get better, Genevieve. I want it so badly. I've never wanted anything so much for so long and made so little progress. I mean, I'm over here patting myself on the back because I've gone thirty-six days. And even that feels like too much already."

Soft but certain, Genevieve says, "Jacob. I'm here for you. I've always been here. You just need to ask."

"No, I know. We always said we'd be a team."

"We *said* that, Jacob. But don't you think you were always trying to fix this on your own? Always Mr. Perfect, can't bear to let anyone down?"

"You sound like Carl."

Genevieve laughs, "I can't help you if you don't let me, Jacob. It's okay to need help. You might be surprised how much people will still like you if you do."

Nothing makes sense, but it's nice to hear her voice. "Yeah. Maybe."

"So what do we do now?"

Jacob thinks for a second.

"I don't even know what I need. This is bigger than me. I think I have to let go of... something. Of being the guy who looks like he has it all together. Maybe I just need to learn to ask."

"Yeah. I think you do. This is good, Jacob."

Maybe it is.

"And come home! I've read that blasted story to Owen fifteen times already, and it's your turn."

Jacob smiles. "Okay. I'm coming home."

Jacob hangs up the phone and sits in the still of the night for a few more seconds. Then he starts the car. But before he backs out, he picks his phone up one more time, taking his last deep breath of the evening.

He opens his contacts and dials Carl.

1   Van der Kolk, Bessel. *The Body Keeps the Score: Brain, Mind, and Body in the Healing of Trauma*. Reprint edition. London: Penguin Books, 2015.

2   Shapiro, Francine. *Eye Movement Desensitization and Reprocessing: Basic Principles, Protocols, and Procedures*. 2nd edition. New York: Guilford Press, 2001.

3   Gottman, John, and Nan Silver. *Seven Principles for Making Marriage Work: A Practical Guide From the Nation's Foremost Relationship Expert*. Revised edition. New York: Harmony Books, 2015.

4   Frost, Robert. "A Servant to Servants." Public Domain, 1915.

5   Rohr, Richard. "Richard Rohr Meditation: Necessary Boundaries." *Center for Action and Contemplation*, 2020 Cac.org/necessary-boundaries-2020-08-10 (accessed January 21, 2021).

6   Saint-Exupéry Antoine de, and Simone Lamblin. *Citadelle*. Paris: Gallimard, 1972.

CONCLUSION:
YOUR HAPPILY
EVER AFTER

It is only ever possible to live happily ever after on a day to day basis.
 —*Margaret Bonanno*

ADAM

I'd like to promise that if you carefully read every word in this book and apply all of our advice, you'll have a perfect marriage, you'll ride off into the sunset, and porn won't ever feature in your life together. But I won't.

We all know life doesn't work like that. Rather, it seems to have a miraculous way of surprising us in the most complicated (and sometimes ironic) ways, testing the very limits of our ability to cope.

Louis Pasteur famously said, "chance favors the prepared mind." Except he said it in French. The point is, preparation can make the difference between accidentally having an okay-ish marriage and intentionally building a great one. We certainly can't predict the future, but when we're prepared for common challenges, life tends to go much better than when we just wing it. Even so, preparation can't save you from the fact that a lot of life is just plain hard.

No matter how your current and future relationships turn out, when you implement what you've read, you'll be stronger and more fearless. Despite other people's choices, you win when you've done the work to become a healthier, more self-aware, more confident person.

WENDY

Of the women we interviewed, some of their relationships worked out, and some didn't. But all of them gained new awareness and perspective as a result of their struggles.

TONYA AND JOHN

Tonya, who we met in Chapter Eight, in her second marriage after an abusive, cheating one, ended up divorced another time, and not by her choice. After five years of marriage and an adorable daughter together, John left her, for reasons not entirely related to his pornography use (although Tonya said it certainly played a role). Tonya's two sons from her previous marriage had a lot of challenges of their own, exes and in-laws brought too much drama and vitriol, and money was tight.

The stress of it all was too much for John, and from Tonya's perspective, he gave up on her and their daughter. Despite the fact that John was kinder and gentler than her first husband, Tonya found herself heartbroken a second time. Tonya hasn't even been able to locate John for the past five months. He's made no attempts to see his daughter as Tonya waits for back child support and struggles to complete the divorce papers. Life is rough and lonely for Tonya, but she hopes to find her happy ending someday. She says she'd love to meet someone who isn't plagued by a pornography habit.

MAGGIE AND BRAD

Single and cancer-free, Maggie's still got her mohawk, although it's black, not pink now. Every time she thinks she might grow it out, she always comes back to it, a symbol of her strength during her battle with breast cancer. She's come a long way from the days when she was married to a man who watched porn twelve hours a day, ran up $800 in secret credit card bills, and only had sex with her six times in ten years.

Maggie's a proud mama. Both of her kids graduated from high school this year. Her daughter worked hard to graduate a year early and is now studying at a hair design school. And her son has a prestigious soccer scholarship at a university back East. Not long ago, Maggie discovered that her breast implants were making her sick, so she made the brave decision to go under the knife one more time for a second and final mastectomy. She feels fantastic, like she has a new lease on life. She just entered the business world and opened a smoothie shop, and she doesn't have a second to herself to think or rest, but she's happy to be on her own two feet and taking care of her family.

She's also passionate about teaching adolescent development and puberty to fifth and sixth graders at schools all over her home state. She wants kids to learn to love their bodies and appreciate the amazing things they can do. She's never looked back on divorcing Brad and still considers it the best choice for herself and her kids.

MONICA AND CHRISTIAN

Monica from Chapter Ten had the long road to find her own healing from trauma in an understanding twelve-step group. She eventually found that surrender for herself, first in a support group outside of her own faith tradition, and then within it.

All that while, Christian slowly worked out his own recovery, continually taking a few steps forward, a few back. When I spoke to her two-and-a-half years later, life had thrown her yet more curveballs, even though I thought she'd already had enough shocks and surprises for one lifetime.

After our first conversation, Christian had months of sobriety under his belt for the first time since he was young. With the help of his therapist, he was preparing a formal disclosure to Monica of all of his behaviors and relapses over the years. She thought he might spend a couple of weeks writing it out, but it took him seven months.

The week before they were scheduled to meet with Christian's therapist for the disclosure, Christian told Monica that she probably wouldn't hear anything she didn't already know. Maybe he was telling himself that was true.

At the disclosure, Monica was shocked to learn that Christian hadn't just acted out with pornography, but that on a few occasions, he had sexual experiences with real people—specifically with men. After twelve years of marriage, Monica had never suspected Christian's attraction to men. And the knowledge that he'd been unfaithful to her devastated Monica.

After learning that, Monica checked into a hotel for three days and spiraled right back into her trauma that had seemed long gone at that point. After all she'd been through, those three days were the worst of her life. She was desperate for surrender but coming up empty. When she returned home, heartbroken, she decided she needed Christian to move out for six weeks so she could have space to sort out her feelings about all of this. When she delivered that news at his next therapy appointment, Monica said it felt like someone else was speaking the words coming out of her mouth— she wasn't the type of person who asked her husband to move out, was she? Christian broke down, sobbing.

But he packed up his stuff, and for the first time in his life told his three children about his struggles with pornography. He said he loved them and would be there for them, even though he and Monica needed to be apart for now. Monica was proud of how he handled that.

Those six weeks turned into nine months. Those were the first months Monica saw Christian start to explore his own recovery. His therapist encouraged him to work to understand his sexuality. With so many of his secrets finally out in the open, Christian could investigate his own life and try to make decisions about it. After those nine months, he confessed to her, "This is what I know: I believe I'm gay, and I've always been gay. Also, I know I want to stay married to you."

He found and connected with a couple in Utah who were living a mixed-orientation marriage. He wanted some guidance from their experience. He went on retreats with other men who wanted to make their mixed-orientation marriages work. Monica said she felt anxious about him spending time with men he might be attracted to. But he always came home speaking openly about his emotions and experiences, something Monica hadn't seen before.

Monica was ready for him to move back home, but she didn't know what life would be like now. A couple weeks after he moved back, they tried going out on a date. This was stressful for Monica. She wanted to cry during dinner and broke down during the movie they went to see afterward.

On the drive home, Christian turned to Monica and asked something he never had before: "How are you doing?"

"He never asked me, because he always knew my answer would make him spiral into his shame again. But this time, he did," Monica told me on our Zoom call three months later.

Monica, taken aback, was slow to answer his question, so Christian pulled the car over to the side of the road. "Let's talk about how you're doing," he said. For Monica, this was a turning point, a revolution maybe. After twelve years of marriage, they really started to talk.

"I can't tell you where we'll be a year from now. I can't even tell you whether we'll be together or not. But these past three months have been the most intimate of my entire marriage. If nothing else, at least Christian is becoming honest with himself and figuring out who he is."

All these unknowns don't come easily to Monica. At forty-one years old, she's five months pregnant with their fifth child, an entirely unexpected turn of events. Security about the future of her relationship would be nice, but she's trying again to surrender to the unknown.

Monica still draws great strength from her online twelve-step meeting with other women of her faith. She also now attends support groups for wives in mixed-orientation marriages. But the ones she's found are all about supporting spouses and taking care of their needs. She hopes to someday find one that gives women strength and resources to meet their own needs, just like those twelve-step meetings that helped her find recovery and peace. Who knows? Maybe fierce, vibrant Monica will start one herself.

MARIANA AND DANNY

Mariana and Danny are still happily married. If you'll recall, she's the busy therapist with two kids, and Danny's the IT guy who found recovery because of his willingness to lay down his will for his higher power.

"I just went to a meeting last night," Danny tells me. He still has the same sponsor who spoke up about his own recovery from porn one fine Sunday at church all those years ago.

Like the rest of us, they've been hunkering down, surviving COVID-19. They're figuring out how to work and raise kids from home. Their eight-year-old son was just diagnosed with autism, which has shaken their world a bit.

"It's good in a lot of ways, because we can get him more resources, more access for the things that he struggles with," Danny says. "But I realize this is one more step in my recovery. I know for me, as a father, realizing how much I don't have control over some of these circumstances—how my son sees the world, how he interacts with me... I mean, the only thing I really have control over is how I respond to my son and how I relate to him. And that's been really challenging. I rationalize in my head that this is what the world's like. 'I want you to learn these skills. I want you to avoid pain and suffering.' Most of that stuff I have to flush down the toilet with our oldest son. Because what I think he needs, more often than not, that's not what he needs. I'm having to apply— No, I'm *getting* to apply a lot of these principles of recovery... to my relationship with my son."

As for Mariana, now that she's recovered from her trauma and no longer feels a pull to obsess about Danny's porn use, she has space to explore parts of herself she's neglected for years, including her Latina identity. "When we first got married, race wasn't something we really talked about. Because I just wanted to blend in. I didn't want to bring attention to the fact that I'm clearly not American or White. But in my experience living here in Utah, it hasn't always been... fun, let's be honest. There's lots of discrimination going on here. So for me, I'm at a point where I can finally say, 'I'm gonna bring these things up.' So I've been learning how to speak on racial justice these past eighteen months."

Danny has begun sponsoring other compulsive porn users searching for recovery and helping out a couple in their neighborhood with their own problems surrounding pornography. He's also had the opportunity to share his story in a church class multiple times, just like his sponsor did all those years ago. "It's not an easy thing to do, but it's something I'm willing to do. I don't have anything to be ashamed of anymore. I used to feel incredible amounts of shame." In many ways, life has come full circle for Mariana and Danny.

ALEX AND LUKE

Then there's Alex, the woman who found comfort in the idea of liminal spaces because she and her boyfriend had been dating exclusively for almost two years, feeling like they were headed nowhere.

After Alex turned down Luke's proposal, she wanted to stay with him, so she started to set up some boundaries that worked for her. When Alex felt anxious about being with Luke, she'd tell him that she needed three days apart, instead of just ending it with him then and there. And she let him know that she couldn't marry someone who can't hold down a job. For his part, Luke started doing his own work to better manage his depression. He learned to be vulnerable and honest with his managers if he was struggling, rather than miss an entire day of work. He found that his boss was understanding if he would only show up and put in the time.

Six months later, on Christmas Day, he proposed again. Alex said yes this time. They married in May and a few weeks later went off to Arizona to spend the summer living the rugged life as counselors at an outdoor program for at-risk youth.

Eight months later, they had me over for broccoli cheese soup at their newlywed apartment. I was happy to finally meet Luke. Two years earlier, he'd been too intimidated to meet with me, so I heard his entire story through Alex. Now he was exuberant and talkative, eager to share what he was learning from the self-help books he was reading and his twelve-step group.

Alex and Luke were both busy with work and school, but they also were making time to be a resource and a listening ear to anyone in their community who was struggling with pornography. "And we're so happy," Alex added that night, two years after we first met. "Our relationship felt like a huge mess at the time, and I was worried it would never get better. But now I'm glad it all happened the way it did."

Eleven months after that, in the midst of a global pandemic, they've both finished school, and Luke is thriving at his dream job he landed in politics. And they've been expecting their first child. And in the way life throws us challenges we can't plan for, Alex just gave birth to that baby boy thirteen weeks before his due date, weighing in at less than two pounds. Alex and Luke have stayed by their baby's side in the NICU for over a month now as the little fighter has received a blood transfusion, been fed through a PICC line, and breathed through a ventilator. But he's growing and weaning off of his many life-saving contraptions as Alex and Luke have grown closer as well. Amidst the sudden grief for the life they'd wanted for their son, Alex says she and Luke couldn't be more in love with their little boy.

PENNY AND EDWIN

And what about Penny and Edwin, the dating couple who got back together after a six-month break? These two dated exclusively for another six months after that. After a year of sobriety, Edwin wanted to get engaged. Penny didn't think they were ready yet. In the end, among other issues such as his inertia toward achieving his life goal of becoming a junior high science teacher, Edwin's struggle to manage his negative moods created overwhelming stress for Penny. Edwin was never rude, mean, or violent, but on more than one Friday afternoon, Penny sat at her desk and cried because she knew that after work she'd be spending the weekend together with Edwin, and she couldn't handle the looming tension from his moods that swung more often than they stabilized.

On the night Penny broke up with Edwin, she was determined to make the right choice for herself. All the same, Penny and Edwin loved each other, and it broke their hearts to let go. They held each other and cried for hours at Penny's apartment until she knew Edwin had to leave, or she'd never let go.

Over the three years since she broke up with Edwin, Penny has dated a couple of other guys. She still attends her recovery group for partners, even though she's single. Although she hasn't formally identified an addiction or trauma of her own, she loves the personal growth and connection to God that twelve-step offers. She attributes that life change to dating Edwin.

For Edwin's part, after he and Penny broke up, he turned straight back to porn to cope with his pain. That went on for a couple of years before he knew this wasn't a life—he needed help. He returned to twelve-step and found recovery again. He met a girl. They're married now.

I had the chance to talk to Penny while she reflected back on it all two years after the big breakup: "I wasn't okay with the way he just lived his life from day to day only, not thinking ahead, not advancing toward a career. He had zero issues with anything about me... just wanted to be loved... and that was childlike and just not what I wanted in a life partner. So I was waiting for him to make a lot of progress in recovery and become more. He needed to do a lot of work on himself to recover from a traumatic childhood.

"And I do want to find the right guy and get married someday. I still believe in love. But I'm happy where I am. I was surprised how relieved I felt after Edwin and I broke up. It would have been so much harder if we were married. And I know I grew from the experience. So I'm grateful it turned out how it did." Penny looks me in the eye and smiles.

Even after all of these follow-up interviews, many of our brave interviewees are still in the middle of their stories, on the side of the road next to their busted post-midnight pumpkin coaches, on the phone with AAA, looking for a tow back into town. So please don't judge the ending by the middle.

Actually, all of our interviewees are in the middle of their stories, even the ones who've found recovery and those who've built healthy relationships. For all of us, there will always be another challenge. Some of them will break our hearts. And there will always be another glorious sunrise, another moment of connection, another reason to rejoice. Wherever we are in our stories, there's more to do and to become.

We can't wave a magic wand and change our ordinary lives into the perfect fairy tale or transform someone we love into the person we wish they were. But maybe that's not what we need anyway. In the end, we might look back and find that life's twists and turns brought us everything we never knew we wanted. Some of our happily ever afters aren't quite what we expected.

GENEVIEVE   JUNE 2017

Standing next to the unmade bed, Genevieve pulls the comforter up over the sheets and smooths it flat with the palms of her hands, making a space for the suitcase, which she then hoists up onto the bed and zips open. In go a pair of sandals and her favorite ballet flats. She reaches for her black polka dot heels, then reminds herself that she only has space for the basics. Next: blouses, jeans, a cotton skirt, a pile of dresses and play clothes for Maya, t-shirts and shorts for Owen, diapers, onesies, pajamas, and shoes for the baby. Genevieve's chest flutters, but her fingers move swiftly and calmly as she plays real-life Tetris with her little family's belongings. She heads to the bathroom to grab her toothbrush, toothpaste, and the lime green hairbrush, the only one that doesn't make Maya squeal in pain when Genevieve passes it through her hair.

Pain. Ooh, Tylenol. If the baby gets an earache, nobody will get any sleep without it. Genevieve heads out toward the kitchen, closing the bedroom door softly behind her and tiptoeing down the hallway. Reaching into the cabinet for the Tylenol, and then grabbing the diaper cream for good measure, she hears Jacob's voice in the living room.

"Yeah, we have three kids. Maya's eight, Owen's six..."

Oh, gosh. Is it 2:00 already? He'll wake the baby. Genevieve rushes around the corner into the living room, finger to her lips, whispering, "Hey, hon, could you—"

"...and this little guy is eighteen months old. His name's Max."

On the couch, Jacob holds Max up by his armpits close to the computer screen that's standing open on the footstool. Max wriggles his dangling legs, his lips curling into a smile as he watches Genevieve enter.

"Oh. I didn't know he was awake. Hi, Buddy!" She coos at Max as she takes him from Jacob's arms and rounds the computer to see the screen. She sees the face of a woman with red frizzy hair looking back at her. "Is this the interview?" she whispers to Jacob.

"Yeah, this is Wendy. She's the one doing the interviews for that book."

"Hi, you must be Genevieve," Wendy's tinny voice says through the screen.

"Oh, hi! I was wondering when we'd get to talk to you."

Jacob turns back to Genevieve. "Max woke up while you were billing vendors, and I didn't want to bug you because you were like, in the zone."

"Oh, gosh. He isn't sleeping at all lately. How are we even going to get over jet lag?"

Jacob motions to Genevieve to sit down next to him. "Come talk to Wendy with me."

"Yeah. I want to. I was planning on it. I just have to finish packing. I'm almost done." Genevieve sits down, then stands up again. "Dang it! Marissa's almost hit ninety days at the store—I have to get her on the insurance plan today." Leaving town starts to feel impossible.

Jacob motions to her again. "Come sit down and talk. I'll fight with the insurance company after we're done. And I'll pack my suitcase and finish yours. You can just pick up the kids from school before we leave."

Genevieve sits down next to Jacob, her leg touching his. He bumps her shoulder with his and flashes her a sneaky smile.

"Are you all going somewhere?" Wendy asks.

"We're flying away to France tonight," Jacob replies, his chest growing big.

"Oh, wow."

"Yeah. We probably sound crazy," Genevieve says.

"This is literally the only thirty minutes we could fit in this week to meet with you," Jacob adds.

"Well, thank you for taking your precious time on a busy day! Sounds like you guys have an exciting life."

"Not really. This is the first time we've gone anywhere other than to visit family. The first time any of us has left the country." He looks over at Genevieve, "The first time the kids have flown on a plane."

"The first time *I've* flown on a plane," Genevieve says, her chest all aflutter again.

Jacob's eyes widen. "That's right!"

Genevieve nods. "I've wanted to see Paris since I was a kid."

"Well, I don't want to take up too much of your time today. This is just a 'get to know you' interview. We'll schedule an interview to document your entire story when you get back. And I *really* appreciate your time and your bravery sharing your story with us. It will help a lot of people in your situation."

"We're happy to do what we can." Jacob pauses, looking across the room at the wall. "I used to be so private about all of this. Terrified of what people would think of me if they knew."

"Well, I'm really glad you're sharing this. You have no idea how many people are in your shoes," Wendy says.

"I've got a pretty good idea," Jacob chuckles, looking down at the baby's head next to him.

"Well, I know that porn is something you've had to confront in your marriage, but I want to know where you're at now, and then we'll work back to the beginning of your story next time."

Jacob takes a deep breath. Genevieve feels like she wants to do the same.

"So where are you guys at right now, recovery-wise? How is your marriage?"

Jacob's voice cuts through the silence. "Yeah, to be honest, it's been a huge problem for us. My choices hurt Genevieve a whole lot. I hated that." His eyes meet Genevieve's. "But recovery has been... It's changed my life. I'm learning to stop making everything about me. And I've been sober for almost two years now, the longest—"

"It's been over two years," Genevieve chimes in.

Jacob squints and half-smiles at Genevieve, "Really?"

"Yes."

Jacob tilts his head to the side.

"Yes!" Genevieve laughs. "It was two years three weeks ago."

"Oh, wow. I haven't been to a meeting in awhile. I'll have to pick up a chip."

"Yeah, you will." Genevieve eyes Jacob.

Genevieve's phone rings in her pocket. She hands Jacob the baby and pulls it out. "It's my mom. I should probably take this before we go."

"It's okay. I'll finish talking to Wendy. You can tell her your story next time."

"Yeah, it was nice to meet you, Genevieve. We'll talk soon," Wendy says.

Genevieve holds the phone to her ear, smiles and nods at the woman on the computer screen, and walks out of the room into the hallway. "Hey, Mom."

"Genevieve. I just had a thought. I heard the drinking water is contaminated in France. I don't want any of my grandbabies—"

"Mom, France is a developed nation. In Paris they pride themselves on the quality of their tap water. We looked it up."

"Well, I've also heard they kidnap American kids abroad."

"Mom. We will be fine. You don't need to worry. Jacob and I will keep the kids safe."

"I know, I know. You're an adult now. You don't need me anymore. It's just that..." Her voice starts to squeak, dissolving into sobs.

"Mom. Mom. Hey. We're going to be okay on our own. I'm busy getting ready for our flight, so I need to go, but we will call you and Dad when we get to France so you know that we're okay."

"Okay, but—"

"Mom. I have to go. I love you, Mom. We love you. It will be okay."

"Okay, Sweetheart. Bye."

Genevieve hangs up and enters the family room again. The laptop is closed now, and Jacob's standing in the middle of the room with his phone wedged between his shoulder and his ear, lifting Max high above his head and then pretending to let go as he lowers him abruptly. Max's deep belly giggles grow with each trip on the Daddy coaster.

"Yes." Jacob abruptly says into the phone. "I need to add an employee to our group plan..." His voice trails off.

"I'm on hold again." He looks over at Genevieve. "Can you believe we're going to Paris?" He raises his eyebrows and smiles. "Yes," he abruptly says back into the phone. He pulls his phone away from his ear and looks at it. "Oh! I have to take this." He presses the screen and puts the phone back to his ear, sitting down on the couch, letting Max wriggle out of his arms and walk away.

"Hey. How're you doing?" He flashes another smile at Genevieve then looks back toward the opposite wall. "No, I'm glad you called. Honestly, calling my sponsor was one of the hardest things at first. How are you doing?"

Genevieve leans against the wall, watching Jacob on the phone.

Two years. The days go by so fast. With the kids, the bookstore, the house, Genevieve hardly has time to stop and think. That's how she and Jacob like it. They work hard for their kids' security and take nothing for granted. But some days her old self feels like a lifetime ago. The old Genevieve, the one who lived her life terrified of some unspoken impending doom, thinking the only way she could save herself was by micromanaging everything— every*one* else. The Genevieve who dreaded every phone call, bracing herself for whatever bad news might be on the other side of the line. The Genevieve who had to hang onto everything she owned, the things she liked and the things she didn't, convinced everything was slipping away.

The old Jacob is gone now too, the one who needed constant validation. The Jacob who always had to be right. Jacob who kept secrets, who hid so much away. Maybe old Jacob was terrified too—that he'd lose all of them if he wasn't Mr. Perfect all the time.

"You've got this. Bye, man." Jacob taps his phone screen again and sets it on the couch, then picks it up again. "I forgot about the insurance company!"

Through the sliding glass door, the branches of the giant oak tree are swaying. Genevieve sits down next to Jacob, wrapping her arms around his waist and burrowing her nose into his shoulder. She feels his lips brush against her forehead, and when she looks up at him, he's got that questioning look.

"What is it?" she laughs.

"We're going to Paris."

"We are."

"Are we ready for this adventure?"

She takes a breath, then exhales, letting it flood to her fingers and toes.

"Ready as we'll ever be."

ACKNOWLEDGMENTS

ADAM

All the way back in 2014, my wife told me she was requiring me to write this book. She said, "I have an idea for a book and no one is going to write it, so you need to do it." From concept to completion, this book took nearly eight years to finish. Every time I wanted to give up, my wife was the engine pushing me forward. Lindsay is the reason my adult life has turned out as well as it has, on every possible level.

This book also wouldn't exist without Wendy. Her dogged tenacity in completing projects and fierce commitment to making the book a thoroughly enjoyable read transformed my dry and clinical manuscript into the beautiful thing it is today.

My parents' dedication to education propelled me to the position of having enough knowledge and expertise to be able to write a book like this. I'm sure I don't thank them enough for everything they've done for me. I'm grateful to Geoff Steurer, my original therapist mentor and the one who started me down the path of treating problematic sexual behaviors so many years ago. I'm thankful to my good friend, Scott Shaffer, for creating the Maslow drawing for the book and for offering feedback on our cover design.

Of course, I'm indebted to the clients who have entrusted their well-being to me over the years and have taught me how people heal. Being a therapist has enriched my life beyond what I could have imagined. More than anything else, this book is a love letter to the gritty souls who have lived the lives described on these pages. Don't ever give up.

WENDY

This book wouldn't be what it is without the courage and

vulnerability of the people who spent hours with me sharing their struggles, triumphs, heartbreak, and redemption. Their stories brought the book to life. I unfortunately can't thank any of them by name here, but they know who they are.

Adam's offer to have me edit this book brought me out of the blissful obscurity of stay-at-home mom life chasing toddlers and changing diapers. His eventual willingness to let me weasel my way into co-authoring with him when I found I was excited about the subject and the difference we could make set my life on a new trajectory. I'm also grateful for his wife Lindsay's friendship and championing of this book.

I'm indebted to my enthusiastic, supportive writers group, the ReVisionaries. In so many ways, they taught me how to be a real writer (if there is such a thing), and they provided invaluable feedback that changed the course of the book. I want to especially thank those who took hours out of their lives to read our manuscript: Sandra Tayler, Mikki Tolley, Hayley Hess-Beaumont, Nicole Brower, Katelyn Brower, Jessica Allred, Heidi Darley, Dominique Burton, Daphne Higbee, and Meg Sherman. Melissa Muhlenkamp and Brittney Wakefield provided insights on our cover design. I'm also grateful to Martha Rasmussen and Deb Goodman for beta reading our manuscript as well. Via her company, Bookaholics Press, Martha worked tirelessly to meet our over-the-top and obsessively nitpicky formatting needs. And most of all, I have to thank Peter and my kids, Anna, Ewan, Cecily, Fiona, Rhyn, and Zippy, for believing in me, for calling me on my bullshit, and for making me laugh when the days get gray.

APPENDIX A:
WRITING ABOUT
YOUR EMOTIONS

Below you'll answer two sets of questions. First, write your feelings about pornography and your relationship. After you have The Talk, write about your feelings again. Notice what has changed and what has stayed the same.

BEFORE THE TALK

The emotions that motivate me to address pornography in my relationship:

_____

_____

_____

My greatest fear(s) about pornography and my relationship:

_____

_____

_____

Relating to pornography and my relationship, I feel peaceful about:

_____

_____

_____

AFTER THE TALK

What my partner said in our conversations that most worried me:

_____

_____

_____

What my partner said that are most comforting to me:

_____

_____

_____

My emotions that surprised me or were different than I expected during The Talk:

_____

_____

_____

The emotions I'm most likely to show and share with others:

_____

_____

_____

The emotions I'm most likely to withhold from others:

_____

_____

_____

The reasons I might not share *all* of my emotions and thoughts:

_____

_____

_____

APPENDIX B:
A GUIDE TO YOUR EMOTIONS
AND FEELINGS

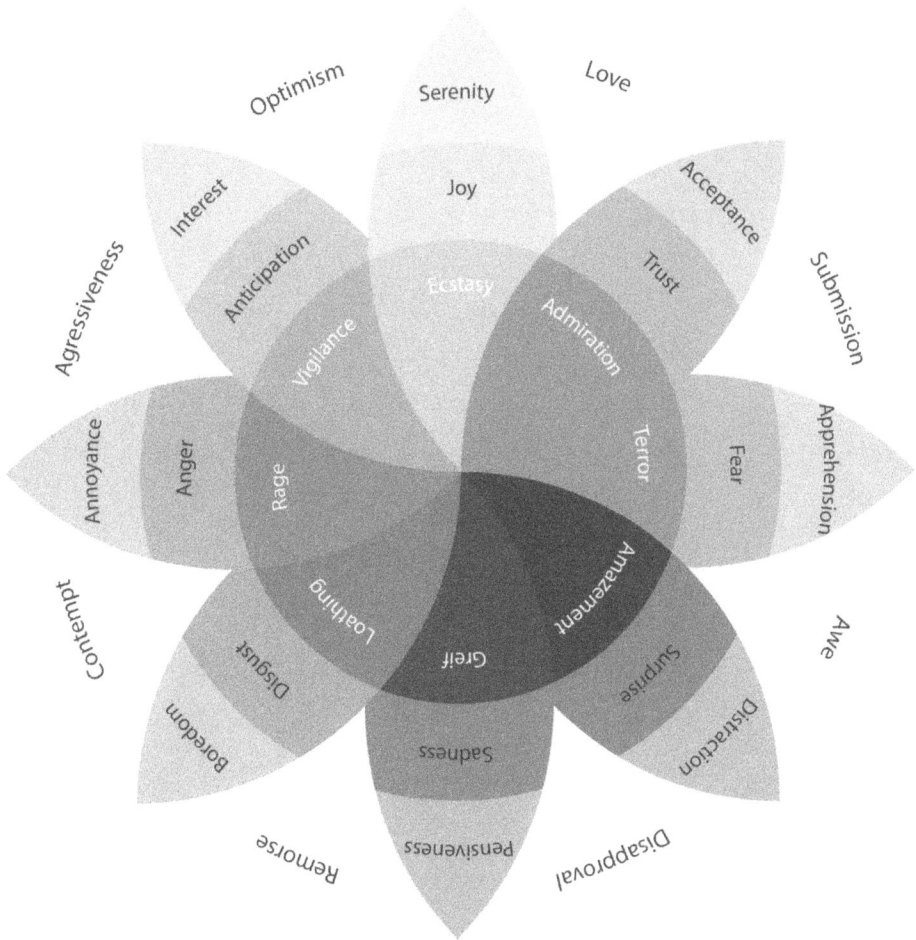

Robert Plutchik's wheel of emotions, developed in 1980

APPENDIX C:
HELPFUL BOOKS

ON SETTING BOUNDARIES

Boundaries in Dating: How Healthy Choices Grow Healthy Relationships by Henry Cloud and John Townsend

Boundaries: When to Say Yes, How to Say No to Take Control of Your Life by Henry Cloud and John Townsend

Boundaries Where You End and I Begin: How to Recognize and Set Healthy Boundaries by Anne Katherine

Set Boundaries, Find Peace: A Guide to Reclaiming Yourself by Nedra Glover Tawwab

ON HEALING FROM TRAUMA

The Body Keeps the Score: Brain, Mind, and Body in the Healing of Trauma by Bessel van der Kolk

How to Do the Work: Recognize Your Patterns, Heal From Your Trauma, and Create Your Self by Nicole le Pera

It Didn't Start With You: How Inherited Family Trauma Shapes Who We Are and How to End the Cycle by Mark Wolynn

Walking the Tiger: Healing Trauma by Peter Levine and Anne Frederick

ON NAMING AND MANAGING EMOTIONS

Feelings Buried Alive Never Die... by Karol K. Truman

How Emotions Are Made: The Secret Life of the Brain by Lisa Feldman Barrett

ON MINDFULNESS AND MEDITATION

Bliss More: How to Succeed in Meditation Without Really Trying by Light Watkins

Mindfulness for Beginners by Jon Kabat-Zinn

Stress Less, Accomplish More: Meditation for Extraordinary Performance by Emily Fletcher

The Surrender Experiment: My Journey into Life's Perfection by Michael A. Singer

The Untethered Soul: The Journey Beyond Yourself by Michael A. Singer

ON TWELVE-STEP RECOVERY

The Big Book of Alcoholics Anonymous by Alcoholics Anonymous World Service, Inc.

Breathing Underwater: Spirituality and the Twelve Steps by Richard Rohr

Recovery: Freedom From out Addictions by Russell Brand (content warning: abundant and gleeful F-bombs)

ON UNDERSTANDING YOUR ACCOUNTABILITY STYLE

The Four Tendencies: The Indispensable Personality Profiles That Reveal How to Make Your Life Better (and Other People's Lives Better, Too) by Gretchen Rubin

ON THE HARMS OF PORNOGRAPHY

The Porn Myth: Exposing the Reality Behind the Fantasy of Pornography by Matt Fradd

Your Brain on Porn: Internet Pornography and The Emerging Science of Addiction by Gary Wilson

ABOUT THE AUTHORS

Adam is a marriage and family therapist, public speaker, and co-owner of a network of outpatient mental health clinics. He has an obsession for learning new skills, completing items on checklists, and spreadsheets. Adam and his wife Lindsay split their time between sunny St. George, Utah and the little farming community of Mapleton, Utah, tending to their counseling offices and their five children (and three dogs).

Wendy works as a writer, editor, and therapist. She has a master's degree in English language from Brigham Young University and an upcoming degree in clinical mental health counseling from the University of Utah. She's passionate about faith, family, friends, and pebble ice. She lives in Mapleton, Utah with her husband Peter, six kids, three cats, a dog, five chickens, and a bunny.

www.ingramcontent.com/pod-product-compliance
Lightning Source LLC
Chambersburg PA
CBHW032123020426
42334CB00016B/1049